**The Sixth Edition**

**of**

# THE HOW BOOK

## For

# GENEALOGISTS

A guide to give the new genealogist a proper start.

A help for the experienced genealogist in the many problems connected with the search for ancestors.

EDITED BY

George B. Everton Sr.

Published by

THE EVERTON PUBLISHERS, INC.

HPO Box 368

LOGAN, UTAH, 84321

*CS16
.E9
1964

LIBRARY OF CONGRESS CATALOG CARD NUMBER
63-23103

SIXTH PRINTING – MARCH 1969

LITHOGRAPHED IN THE U.S.A.
KEITH WATKINS & SONS, INC.

BINDING BY
MOUNTAIN STATES BINDERY

# FOREWORD

The idea of "The How Book" came to the late Walter M. Everton while engaged as an advisor to people interested in genealogical research around San Francisco. He found that scores of inquiries coming to him daily centered around a number of specific topics. Finding he was writing the same kind of a letter several times a day in answer to inquiries, he decided to mimeograph each letter he wrote on any particular phase of genealogy. Eventually he had seventy-three different short letters. From two to five of these different letters were sent to each one of the twenty or more daily inquiries. Returning to his home in Logan, Utah, in 1945, he founded the genealogical section of the Cache County Library. When inquiries continued to come from near and far from bewildered researchers he decided to combine his letters into a three-and-a-half by eight-and-a-half mimeographed, "The How Book For Genealogists." It contained seventy-eight pages. The demand for this little pamphlet was enormous.

The 1948 edition of this work was a letterpress pamphlet, four by seven. "Revised and enlarged" it sold for twenty-five cents per copy. In each new edition additional information was incorporated of help to the professional as well as the amateur researcher. A total of sixteen thousand copies were distributed throughout the nation.

Sensing that more information was needed to guide the researcher than was given in his "How Book," Mr. Everton conceived the idea of "The Handy Book for Genealogists," the first edition of which was printed in 1949. It included, besides all the material of the "How Book," a section on "Genealogical Geography," and two other sections, "The Directory of Genealogists" and "The Genealogists's Exchange."

Since 1947 he had also published "The Genealogical Helper" a magazine which was first distributed as a monthly and then as a larger quarterly. Immediately after the publication of "The Handy Book for Genealogists" in 1949 it became obvious to Mr. Everton that the two sections in that book, "The Directory of Genealogists and "The Genealogist's Exchange" were of such tremendous importance to the researcher that they must come out with fresh contents at least once a year. Realizing the impossibility of producing a yearly ten thousand edition of "The Handy Book." Mr. Everton decided to incorporate those two sections in the quarterly magazine.

He was making preparation for the "First Annual Exchange Edition" of "The Genealogical Helper" in December 1950 when he was stricken by a fatal heart attack. Since then the Everton Publishers with George B. Everton, Sr., as owner and editor, have tried to emulate his efforts of "helping more people find more genealogy."

The 1953 edition of "The Handy Book for Genealogists" was published by The Everton Publishers with George B. Everton, Sr. and Gunnar Rasmuson as editors. It followed the plan of the original "Handy Book" with some additional information and corrections. Next came "The Third Edition of the Handy Book for Genealogists." It did not contain the "Directory of Genealogists" nor the "Genealogist's Exchange" as they have continued to appear in each September issue of "The Genealogical Helper." Neither did it contain the general instructions incorporated into this book, but it had much additional information on the 48 states with a map of each showing county boundries and much new data on most of the European countries.

The Fourth Edition "The Handy Book for Genealogists" was published in 1962. Many corrections were made in this edition and an attempt was made to standardize the "formation date" of counties, using the date of the legislative act rather than the date the records were started or the officers were elected, as had been done by some authorities of the past. New maps of all the states with their counties were printed in this edition and the counties of bordering states were also shown to assist one in tracing migrations across state lines. Other new additions were "The Genealogists' Check List of Historical Records Survey" and a list of records held by many of the county clerks or clerks of the courts of many counties. All these additions, corrections and changes have proven to be effective helps for all in quest of ancestorial records.

Between 1948 and 1956, while the "How Book" was out of print, seldom a week passed without someone ordering a copy. This continual demand, coupled with new plans and ideas which had been worked out and proven of great help to those interested in genealogical research and the gathering and writing of family and personal histories, finally brought forth the "New How Book for Genealogists." Ten thousand copies were printed and are now in the hands of genealogists all over the world.

Ten thousand copies of the "Improved How Book for Genealogists" published in 1959 were also printed. It had a plastic cover and spiral binding, and had many additions to the "Dictionary of Genealogical Words, Terms and Abbreviations."

George B. Everton, Sr. and Gunnar Rasmuson were co-editors of "The New How Book for Genealogists" and "The Improved How Book for Genealogists."

This "The Sixth Edition of The How Book for Genealogists" is humbly presented. In it we have again added to the "Dictionary" many words and abbreviations to assist you in solving some of the puzzles which may confront you as you try to interpret old or modern genealogical records. We have extended some of the instructions and have added suggestions and recommendations on the use of several new genealogical record-sheets which we have recently developed. All this has been done with a sincere desire to continue the dedication which Walter M. Everton gave to "The Genealogical Helper" - "to assist more people to find more genealogy."

As you read this book you will undoubtedly find mistakes. You can give a helping hand

to us and many other genealogists if you will
let us know about these imperfections. Your
suggestions and comments will also be welcome to help us to plan for future editions.
George B. Everton, Sr., Editor

# INTRODUCTION

Family tree research is one of the most interesting, pleasurable and gratifying hobbies to which you can turn. Following the trails and trials of your forebears can lead you to many exciting tales of successes, trimphs, failures, loves and pathos - true life stories as glamorous as any from Hollywood.

It can also take you to new lands and places, through study and writing, or in person, as you search for the records of your unknown progenitors. You will also broaden your knowledge of history, geography, laws, customs and life in general of the present and the dim past as you delve into records in new and ancient archives.

You will thrill time and time again as you find the accounts of your forefathers' doings - births, marriages, deaths, wills, land transfers, moves, etc. Sometimes you'll run into puzzles as interesting and hard to explain as it is possible to imagine. You will solve some quickly, others may keep you in suspense for years.

How to get started is the big question with most people. What to do first? How to carry on? Where will I find the records of my people? How and what should I record when I do find them? These questions and many others are answered or explained in THE HOW BOOK FOR GENEALOGISTS. It will start you in the proper way and open up hundreds of avenues for you to follow that you may find and record the vital facts and interesting sidelights of your foreparents.

The Everton Publishers have been helping genealogists since before 1947. Besides THE HOW BOOK FOR GENEALOGISTS they also publish THE GENEALOGICAL HELPER, a quarterly magazine, THE HANDY BOOK FOR GENEALOGISTS and many sheets and forms to help you record your family data.

THE GENEALOGICAL HELPER is published each March, June, September and December. It was started in 1947 by the late Walter M. Everton and now has subscribers in every state in the nation and many foreign countries. Thousands have advertised their genealogical problems in its columns and received the solutions from other genealogists who have contacted them after reading the ads. Countless unknown, distant cousins of far-away climes have made contact with each other and then corroborated their efforts in their searches for ancestors, through the pages of this widely read ancestral research magazine.

It can help you in your search whether you are just starting or have had a lot of experience in this enchanting hobby. First you should check recent issues to see who might be interested in your lines. Then you should advertise your wants so others will know of your problems and give you assistance.

Reviews of new publications and stories of various genealogical activities are printed in each issue as well as other guides, helps and instructions for all family tree searchers.

The phenomenal growth of this publication attests that it is living up to its dedication "to help more people find more genealogy."

THE HANDY BOOK FOR GENEALOGISTS, now in its fourth edition is probably the most widely used genealogical book ever published. It gives the formation history of every county in the U.S. and much information regarding their vital records. Brief state histories are also given enabling you to quickly know where you might go or write to get information regarding your ancestors.

State maps showing its counties as well as the counties of bordering states makes it possible for you to easily trace migrations, one of the inevitables of ancestor research. Much information is also given on most of the Western European Countries, showing you many steps to take in your research across the Atlantic.

You will undoubtedly make this book your constant research companion as thousands of professional and amateur genealogists are now doing around the world.

This, THE HOW BOOK FOR GENEALOGISTS is not only designed to give you a start along the ancestor trail - telling you how to begin and how to continue - but it also has many other helps for the long-time genealogist and the newest neophite. You will find in it a relationship chart as easy to read as a mileage chart, showing kinships to ninth cousins, and a formula to figure relationships as far as you may wish to go. "Cousinships" and "times removed" lose their mystery with the easy to understand explanations given in this widely recognized guide for primogenitor searchers.

Another feature of the "How Book" you will use many times is its Dictionary of Words, Terms and Abbreviations. Here are listed and explained hundreds of seldom understood words and terms, local and foreign, used in recording genealogical data. They are all arranged alphabetically to assist you and save you time. You will use this book as long as you do research on your family tree.

You need GENEALOGICAL FORMS to help you record your findings. The charts and forms from The Everton Publishers will give you an assist in making your records clear, understandable, convenient to check and add to. They will also aid you in preserving your records for the future and give you justifiable pride and satisfaction when you display them.

Catalogues are availabe - free of charge - listing all the above and many more instruction books and other aids for genealogical and heraldic enthusiasts. Send for yours now. Just drop a card to: THE EVERTON PUBLISHERS, INC., HPO Box 368, Logan, Utah, 84321.

# TABLE OF CONTENTS

# I
# How To Begin

So you are interested in gathering information about your ancestors? You are not alone with this idea -- genealogy is fast becoming a most popular hobby. Lack of tools and instructions on how to use them - such as forms, binders, etc. - have deterred many from taking up this interesting pastime. Gradually, however, these obstacles are being overcome. With the printing of this book one more step has been accomplished to assist those who desire to occupy themselves in this avocation.

As suggested, one of the first things needed is tools with which to work. Many genealogical forms are now available. As these instructions proceed several will be introduced. If you would like a complete set of sample forms, send 85¢ to The Everton Publishers, Inc., HPO Box 368, Logan, Utah, 84321. Ask for Sample Kit HK2 - 85¢. A free catalogue of genealogical supplies will also be sent.

First is the Family Group Sheet. This is the base or foundation of all genealogical forms. From the information recorded on the

Family Group Sheet other necessary genealogical forms can be started and completed.
On that sheet, when it is properly done, you
have not only the names of your ancestors
or relatives, but also the time, place and
relationship elements which are almost as
essential as the name for proper identification of persons. Many names considered
uncommon today may be found in abundance
in certain localities in past years. Unless
you can connect some dates with those names
– tell where and when they were born, where
and when they were married, where and
when they died, and show their relationship
to other persons – their identity is in-
complete. It may sometimes happen that with
all this information available there may
still be a question of being the same person
because of conflicting information.

Never be satisfied to gather names only.
They may mean something to you today because of your personal acquaintance with
them, but to your descendants in years to
come, they will mean nothing without the
mentioned identifying particulars.

Thus you can see the importance of the
Family Group Sheet. Different kinds of these
sheets are available. Some researchers
prefer one kind, others a different kind. As

long as it contains the needed information, one kind is as good as another. To satisfy individual desires, The Everton Publishers have available five different kinds of Family Group Sheets, designated as A1, F1, F2, F3, and F6. Other forms may be had from other sources. Undoubtedly you may find all necessary forms at the store where you purchased this book. They may not have the same designation as we have given here but they may still be just about the same form, with little or no change. All of them are more or less alike. Therefore, the instructions to be given in these pages just about cover the entire field.

Form A1 is a recent development of The Everton Publishers for forefather searchers who want to use the standard $8\frac{1}{2}$ x 11 inch paper punched for the three-ring binder. It has lines corresponding to the regular typewriter spacing and has spaces for recording more information than most of the forms printed for this purpose. In addition to the usual headings for recording birth, marriage and death dates and places, it also has spaces for occupation, places of residence, church affiliations and military service, etc.

Several other new forms have been printed to be used with the Form A1 in the three-ring binder, including pedigree charts and data work sheets of various kinds. Each will be discussed with their related forms.

Forms F2 and F3, measuring 8½x11, are identical except the paper on which they are printed. Form F3 is printed on a high grade rag bond paper that is not easily torn and will last for many years. Form F2 is printed on a not so heavy sulphite paper that may not withstand the ravages of time and turn yellow with age. Since Form F3 is intended for your personal records it is punched to be preserved in a binder. Form F2, intended mainly as a work sheet in preparation for the long-time-to-be-saved records, is printed on a lighter weight, unpunched paper. It may also be used in sending or asking for information from other researchers.

Form F6 measures 8½x14 and is punched to fit the regular or deluxe binders. It is printed on rag bond, as F3 and F1, but it has more room for recording data.

Form F1 is similar to Form F3 only that it measures 8½x14 and in the extra space are recorded certain ordinances of the Church of Jesus Christ of Latter-day

Saints.  Members of that church would do
well in using the F1, others undoubtedly
would prefer the A1, F3 or F6.  Form **F2**
can be used as a work sheet by either group.

Substantial and attractive loose-leaf binders to fit A1, F1, F3 or F6 can be supplied
from the Everton Publishers or from most
of the stores which sell this book.  Many
other forms mentioned in these instructions
will fit either the one or the other of these
two binders. You may purchase three-ring
binders at any office supply house and most
grocery and drug stores.  Write to the
Everton Publishers for a free catalogue
listing the special binders, the above sheets
and many other genealogical aids.

STARTING YOUR RECORD

The correct way to gather a genealogical
record is to start with your own family.  If
you are married, make out form F2 for the
husband, wife and children. This you should
be able to do from memory or from recent
records made in the Family Bible or elsewhere.  Answer each blank to be filled as if
you were doing it for some one entirely unacquainted with your family.  If you are not
absolutely sure of the dates, don't rely on
your memory.  (Good genealogists prove

every date, place and name with contemporary records, such as birth, marriage and death certificates, Bible, court and census records, old diaries, etc.) Spell all names correctly. In giving the names of your children, list them in order of birth. If a child has died, list it in the order where it belongs, just as you do the living children. Use the child's real name -- not a pet name or nickname

If at all possible, use a typewriter in filling out the record. If a typewriter is not available, print the information in legible style. Don't trust your handwriting -- when it gets cold or is read by a stranger it may be misinterpreted. When writing dates, do it the professional way -- day, month, year -- 10 June 1889. A little time in practice along this line will pay big dividends in the future -- both in time and satisfaction.

Write all names in their regular order -- Christian name first, then the middle name if any, and then the surname (John Christian Jones). Or you may prefer to list the surname first in capitals followed by a comma, then the given names with only the first letter capitalized (JONES, John Christian). Which ever style you use be consistant.

Don't use one style on one sheet and another on the next. The same should apply to all phases of your records, choose a style and stay with it.

Never use initials unless it is impossible to find the name. Rarely you will find someone who was given as his name initials only such as "R" "L" Smith. In such cases, naturally, you must use the initials, since that's all given. When you record an unusual name, underline it showing that you know it to be correct or in the case of initials for names, place them in quotes ("R" "W" etc.). If a person is widely known by a nickname or a legally assumed or adopted name, it is well to place it within parenthesis on the record in connection with the true or original name, as, for instance, John (Jack) Jones, Mary (Polly) Smith, Thomas Polk (Paulk), Henry Black (Schwartz). Don't abbreviate names or persons or localities, with the exception of the officially accepted abbreviations of states. (See p 11).

The spelling of names is another difficulty you will encounter as you follow your ancestor trails. It is not too unusual to find the name of a person spelled differently each time it is recorded. Illiterate persons have had to rely on clerks and other recorders to spell their names. It depended on how the clerk was trained and how it sounded to him as to how he spelled it. Modern spelling methods have also had their influence on surnames. Here is a good rule to follow in most cases: Use the spelling of a person's name as you find it in the earliest record of that person. If you find it spelled other ways later on and wish to show the changes, place as many different spellings as you wish after the first spelling in parenthesis. Of course you may find cases where you will want to deviate from this rule, but show the various spellings to show why you have changed.

On all genealogical records the names of females should be the maiden name only. You will avoid a lot of confusion if you adhere strictly to this rule. Regardless how many times a woman may have been married, use her maiden name only. You will notice there is a space for the names of other husbands she may have had. If her maiden name is unknown, but her given name is known, write it, for instance, Mrs. Bertha Cowles, or if the husband's and the children's surname is known and her names are entirely unknown, write it, for instance, Mrs. John Cowles.

After you have made out your immediate Family Group Sheet make out a similar sheet for the family of the husband's parents, then one for the family of the wife's parents. If you have married brothers and sisters make out Family Group Sheets for each one of them, being careful that all names and dates are correct. If you are not sure of names or dates call them on the telephone or write them for the information. Next make out family group sheets for the families of your parents' brothers and sisters. Be just as careful to get all names and dates on those sheets correct as you were with your own record.

You will find this experience will give you as much satisfaction as any other phase of genealogy. It will also train you in gathering facts and recording them correctly. It will give you such an insight into research activities that by the time you are ready to prepare the records of your grandparents and great grandparents you'll feel like a professional researcher. You will thus have a better insight into what and how to do more complicated situations as you get more and more into the distant past.

As previously mentioned, a good habit to form is to write all dates with the day first, then the month and the year. Never indicate the month with numerals, as 7-12-1893 or 12-7-1893, but always 12 July 1893. Various parts of the world use different numeral systems as dates. This leads to confusion and errors. All the months may be abbreviated to three letters with the exception of June and July and they should be written in full. The year should never be abbreviated. Genealogical dates cover all centuries. To eliminate the century and write '95 instead of 1695, or 1795, or 1895 would be perplexing indeed.

The two lines following the name of the husband and wife records the date and place of birth and the date and place of christening. Both of these dates are not necessary. The date and place of birth is the most important, although, if it is not obtainable, the christening date and place may be substituted. In olden days the clergy often neglected to register the birth of the child, but made note of the christening date when the child was brought to the church for that ordinance. Regarding the time and place of death and the time and place of burial, it would be well if you could get all this information. The death date is the most important but the burial date and place may give you many additional clues.

## ABBREVIATIONS MAY BE BEWILDERING

Abbreviations of names of persons or localities should be avoided. For instance, S. A. may stand for South America, South Africa, South Australia, Santa Ana, Saint Augustine, San Antonio, or San Angelo. While you know perfectly well what you would have the initials represent, to all others they would be an enigma. Your record should withstand the eye of the critic and the test of time. Therefore, use the full name of the town or city, the county, province, shire, canton or lan, and the nation. States in the United States may be abbreviated or not abbreviated according to the Postal Guide, as follows:

| | | | |
|---|---|---|---|
| Ala. | Ind. | Nebr. | S.C. |
| Alaska | Iowa | Nev. | S.Dak. |
| Ariz. | Kans. | N.H. | Tenn. |
| Ark. | Ky. | N.J. | Tex. |
| Calif. | La. | N.Mex. | Utah |
| Colo. | Maine | N.Y. | Vt. |
| Conn. | Md. | N.C. | Va. |
| Del. | Mass. | N.Dak. | Wash. |
| Fla. | Mich. | Ohio | W.Va. |
| Ga. | Minn. | Okla. | Wis. |
| Hawaii | Miss. | Oreg. | Wyo. |
| Idaho | Mo. | Pa. | |
| Ill. | Mont. | R.I. | |

## A FAMILY GROUP SHEET
## FOR EACH MARRIAGE

In these days of divorces it is not un-common to find persons who have been married more than once. In the early days, the rigors, dangers and disease of pioneer life caused homes to be broken and the be-reaved spouse to secure a new companion. The proper procedure in recording these multiple marriages poses problems to the embryo genealogist. However, there is nothing particularly difficult in the situation, if you remember that for each married couple there must be a Family Group Sheet. For each wife, each husband must have a separate Family Group Sheet on which must be shown the children of that marriage, if any.

Part of the information asked for under the ''Husband's Name'' on each Family Group Sheet says, ''Other Wives, if any.'' If the husband has only had one wife, that particular line should remain blank. If the husband in question has had the misfortune to loose two wives and married a third, this notation should be given on that line of the sheet showing the name and data of his first wife, Other Wives, if any, (2) Place maiden name of second wife; (3) Place

maiden name of third wife. On the sheet
showing the information concerning his
second wife, that line should show, (1)
Place maiden name of first wife; (3) Place
maiden name of third wife. On the sheet
showing the information concerning his third
wife, that "Other wives" line should read,
(1) Place maiden name of first wife; (2)
Place maiden name of the second wife.
Following are examples of the above.

Husband's Name, John Jones
Other Wives, if any, (2) Mary Smith, (3)
  Jane Roe
Wife's Maiden Name, (1) Anna Brown

Husband's Name, John Jones
Other Wives, if any, (1) Anna Brown, (3)
  Jane Roe
Wife's Maiden Name, (2) Mary Smith

Husband's Name, John Jones
Other Wives, if any, (1) Anna Brown, (2)
  Mary Smith
Wife's Maiden Name, (3) Jane Roe

Thus, with the three sheets you will be
able to record the children of each marriage, placing them with the proper mother.
By using the number in parenthesis each
time with each wife you eliminate all

questions regarding their order. It may also be well to place the date of the marriage between the name and the number -- (2) 16 May 1810 Mary Smith -- (3) 12 June 1816 Jane Roe -- to make sure there is no question as to the order of marriage.

The same procedure concerning her husbands should be indicated in the wife's information, if she has been married more than once.

The Family Group Sheet is compiled to help you remember at a glance the individuals who are your direct ancestors. In the part where the children of the family are listed, place an asterisk (*) in front of the name of your direct ancestors. It naturally follows, of course, that the husband and wife mentioned on that particular sheet are also your ancestors. It may happen that two children on one Family Group Sheet may be your ancestors. For instance, on one such sheet in our possession, the second child became one of our fifth great grandmothers on our mother's side, and the tenth child became one of our fourth great grandfathers on our father's lineage. An asterisk (*) is placed in front of each one of those two names on that Family Group Sheet of ten children.

How should adopted children be recorded on the Family Group Sheet? After the names of such children write (Adopted). If their blood parents are known, list them on the back of the sheet. It would also be well to make out another Family Group Sheet so that their true brothers and sisters may be shown with them. If the parents are unknown, state that fact. Remember, if possible, blood lines are the ones to follow in tracing genealogy; adopted lines are secondary.

## RECORD THE TRUTH

Sooner or later, a majority of those who do genealogical research find ''skeletons in the closet.'' They discover illegitimacy in their line or other infractions of the law. Considering the practices during the period of time in question this shouldn't be too disturbing or too shocking. Under such conditions paternity is difficult to prove. Rumors and traditions are poor foundations on which to build a pedigree. There is no need to create a scene, to make unnecessary displays. Better far to be quiet, to forget. However, you have more than likely come to the end of that particular lineage. But there is nothing to hinder you from continuing the search on all other lines. Although it may be unsavory, record the truth, but avoid making it prominent. Don't go into detail about such matters. You will find plenty of things to record of which you will be proud.

Mention has been made that sources of information should be recorded. A space for that purpose is reserved on the front of the Family Group Sheet. If that space is insufficient, list all important data on the back of the sheet. (You may also want to record the number of your Form A4, if you are using this method of compiling your data.) Cross references always help in checking and rechecking your records. Many times judgment must be exercised in relation to the interpretation of obscure facts. Your opinion may differ from that of other persons. Give every one a chance to decide for himself by letting him know the source of your information, such as: Family or Bible records (indicate location of the records); U. S. Census records (name year, state, county, etc.); family histories (by whom written and published); State Vital Statistics, etc. This, as has been mentioned, is referred to as the "Historical Method". It is a lot easier than the "Legal Method" perhaps, but not so conclusive.

In the upper right hand corner of the F1, F2 and F6 Family Group Sheets is a place for recording the names of the husband and the wife. As your book grows you will find it convenient to have those names in that position to aid you in locating desired sheets as you thumb through the binder.

## PICTURES WILL
## ENHANCE YOUR RECORD

One of the most interesting phases of genealogy is the gathering of pictures and mounting them with the family record -- practically bringing the family group alive. This is not too difficult with the living, but the farther back you go on your record the more the hardships multiply until you finally reach the time of no photos and few portraits. Some researchers have been able to locate pictures for five or six generations on all their lines. When such an array of photographs is added to the family record it is truly a wonderful sight.

Many ways have been devised for sorting, classifying and mounting pictures. To aid you and give you a start, we will discuss a simple method, then you can add to it, change it or elaborate on it to your heart's content.

Plain sheets are available for mounting your photos and other material you may want to preserve in your record. The S6 sheet, sold by The Everton Publishers, is 8½x14 heavy weight bond paper especially made for mounting. The S7 sheet is the same except for size, measuring 8½x11. Both are punched to fit binders. The A8 and A9 sheets are also 8½x11 but are punched for the three-ring binders. The A8 is heavy like the S6 and S7 and the A9 the same weight as the S4 and S5. Some people have used the S4, S5 and A9 sheets and found them satisfactory, but they are lighter weight, and most people prefer the heavier paper for their permanent records. The lighter weight sheets are used mostly to write histories, other corroborative or interesting material regarding antecedants. As with other sheets you may find just what you need at the store where this book was purchased. You may also be interested in the new acetate sheets which are used to cover the mounted pictures or other valuable records. They may be had in the 8½x14 size, punched to fit the special binders or the three-ring binders. The added protection and beauty they give make them well worth their slight cost.

As with your regular recording activities it is a good idea to start your picture

mounting with your own immediate family.
Place a plain bond sheet on top of your
Family Group Sheet. Turn the plain sheet
over so it will be on your left as you face
it and your Family Group Sheet is on your
right. Paste your family picture on the
plain sheet -- thus when you open your
book after it is assembled you will have
your family group sheet and your picture
sheet so they can be viewed together without
having to turn a page. With pen and ink
print the names of the individuals on the
sheet under the picture - or type them --
in such a way that a stranger could identify
each. Why identify those in the picture so
carefully, since you are intimately acquainted with them? You'll never forget who they
are! That's true, but twenty-five years
from now and later when your descendants
are looking at that picture they may not know
any of them. What wouldn't you give now if
grandma had identified pictures by writing
the names on the back of each. As it is,
there isn't a mark of any kind to identify
the photographed person and the picture
is worthless to you. Learn a lesson from it.
Identify your pictures right now and write
the names of each person from left to right,
top to bottom. Your descendants will bless
you for it! You may also desire to in-
crease interest in the picture by indicating

when it was taken and giving other pertinant data about it. You may even have a story regarding the circumstance of its being taken which would add color. If you have several pictures of the family or individuals in question taken at different times arrange them on the same sheet. You may even have enough picutres to fill both sides of the sheet, or you may prefer to use more sheets and mount pictures on one side only. Reserve space for additional pictures you may obtain later. Let us remind you again -- always identify every individual on every picture you post.

Other interesting material may be included such as birth certificates, wedding announcements, marriage licenses, graduation certificates, discharge papers, newspaper clippings, etc., etc. Anything that is or may become interesting will add value to your record. You may have some treasured bits of cloth, locks of hair, old train tickets, a child's first art work, old letters and other material which does not lend itself to being pasted on the sheet. You may paste a No.10 envelope, or larger, on the sheet and place many of these little heirlooms in it.

## USE RUBBER CEMENT
## OR PHOTO MOUNTING TISSUE

Ordinary paste is rather poor for mounting pictures. It wrinkles the paper and spoils the looks of the finished job. It has a tendency to stiffen, breaking the paper or the picture. Rubber cement will eliminate both of these troubles -- it is always pliable and leaves no wrinkles. It can be purchased at most office supply houses. Another good method for mounting pictures is that used by professional photographers. They use what is called photo mounting tissue -- a thin tissue with shellac on both sides. This is cut to the size of the picture. The tissue is placed on the sheet where you desire it; the picture is placed over it. An electric iron, warm enough to melt the shellac, is placed over the picture. It should remain long enough to melt the shellac, but be careful not to burn the picture. When cooled, the shellac hardens and makes a good bond. Photo mounting tissue in varied sizes may be obtained from photo supply houses.

Snapshots as well as formal pictures will add much to your record. The snapshots will give little or no mounting difficulty but some of the formal pictures may present problems, especially old pictures. For instance, you may find an old group picture of your grandfather's family which is too large to go into your book. These can be copied and reduced to make them usable.

Any professional photographer will do that kind of work. If you are a handy do-it-yourself fellow here's a suggestion. Prop up the picture somewhere out in the sun. Get as close to it as you can with your kodak or cheap box camera and still stay in focus. Shoot the picture just as you would any snapshot. A little experimenting will soon teach you how close you can get and still be in focus. We've seen quite satisfactory results from this method. Those two methods are, perhaps, the extremes in photo copying. Lying between these are the vast resources of the clever amateur photographer with a variety of equipment and devices. Do it yourself or let your professional photographer do it. Use any method you like but never neglect any opportunity to enrich your genealogical record just because some of the available pictures are too large.

Photo copying also comes in handy when you find a rare old picture and the owner refuses to part with it. Have a copy made of it -- there is absolutely no danger of harming the picture since only ordinary photo processes are used.

## PICTURE PEDIGREES

Sometimes you may want a copy of only

one person in a group picture. Take the picture to a professional photographer and he will make the copy of the desired individual in what ever size you may indicate. If you wish to do the work yourself follow previous instructions. After the print is made you can trim away everything but the part you seek.

Copying one face from a group picture becomes a necessity when you are making up a picture pedigree. This is also a most interesting phase of genealogy. For instance, start it with your children, then father and mother, grandparents and great grandparents and so on back as far as you can go. Form P22 is a picture pedigree sheet for use in our 9x15 binders, A6 is designed for the three-ring binders. Or you may wish to use one of the plain heavy sheets and arrange them along your own ideas. We have seen them so arranged and then photocopied so that other members of the family may obtain them if they desire.

For your own or close relative picture groups you may want to arrange them in special sections, such as "Babyhood," "Schooldays," "Hobbies." "Married Life," "Travels," "Friends" etc. Each section may be divided by the use of separation sheets, which may be decorated with cut-out highly colored flowers and/or as much art work as your ingenuity permits. Guide Sheets for Book of Remembrance to fit the 9x15 binders are available from the Everton Publishers and other supply houses.

## CLEAN OLD PHOTOS

Proper handling of old photos will enhance their appearance. Quite often they are blotched and dirty. To clean them, dip a cotton pad in turpentine or ''PM Solution'' and rub vigorously. Turpentine may be purchased at paint stores, ''PM Solution'' at photo supply houses.

Many old photos are mounted on heavy cardboard. If you are going to have a copy made, there is no need to disturb the backing, just clean the photo as suggested. If you contemplate mounting the original photo on one of the sheets in your book, you will find it can be handled much better if the backing is removed. To do this, take a sharp knife; insert it into one of the corners of the backing and tear away the corner to the back of the picture. Catch the edges along the torn part and continue to tear to the back. Repeat until you have enough of the cardboard backing removed to make the picture pliable and suitable for cementing to the plain sheet. Never try to run a knife or other sharp object under the picture or try to lift it from the backing. If you do, you will more than likely ruin it -- the only picture of its kind that is accessible to you. If you have a picture of little value it will be well to do a little practicing before trying it on a picture of greater value. By using this method it will only take you about two or three minutes to strip the backing off any of these old pictures. After the backing is removed you may find it desirable to trim the picture to fit it to the space on the page or to remove superfluous sections.

## THE PEDIGREE CHART

Many people unacquainted with research activities have looked on the pedigree sheet as the most important genealogical record. It does have its place, but in some respects is not so important as the family group sheet. The pedigree chart shows only part of the family record. From the Family Group Sheet comes the information for the pedigree sheet. However the pedigree chart is a good index of the research accomplishments on direct ancestral lines. In other words, in the pedigree chart you have a record showing direct ascent or descent. It does not show brothers and sisters, but parents, grandparents and great grandparents. And still, brothers and sisters are important factors in the identification of the family. They are shown on the Family Group Sheet.

After you have done considerable research work and have located most of your ancestors, say to the fourth and fifth generation, your pedigree chart becomes a guide for your future research. The fan-shaped ten generation pedigree chart, Form P12, with spaces for 1022 names of direct ancestors, is especially designed for that purpose. If you keep that chart abreast with your research continuously, a glance at it will tell you immediately in which direction you should devote your research activities. It measures 22x26 inches, and folds to 8½x14 inches so you can preserve and keep it ever handy in your binder.

Several kinds of pedigree charts are available from the Everton Publishers and other stores carrying genealogical supplies. The P1, P3 and the P11 are for the 9x15 binder. The P1 takes five generations -- names of thirty-one ancestors. Each sheet is arranged so that the pedigree may be continued for any number of generations simply by adding more sheets. The P3 measures 14x25 inches but folds into 8½x14 and is punched to fit the 9x15 binder. Eight generations may be listed on the sheet -- 255 names.   The P11 is 20x25, folds to 8½x14 and is also punched for the 9x15 special binder. You may record nine generations -- 511 names -- on it. Form P2 is a duplicate of P1 but is printed on lighter weight pink paper and is intended only as a work sheet. It can also be used in sending and receiving information through the mails.

Form P7 is a pedigree sheet designed for the 9x12 special binder. It lists five generations -- thirty-one names and has the similar system for extending the pedigree on following sheets as mentioned previously concerning the P1.   The P1 and P7 are printed on heavy rag bond paper, punched for their respective binders.   The P8, a work sheet for the P7, is printed on a light weight sulphite paper and is not punched. Also available for the 9x12 binder is Form P10, 20x25 inches, large enough to handle nine generations.

Form P4, measuring 19x23 inches, lists eight generations, 255 names. It is more of a display chart to demonstrate on one sheet as many of your ancestors as possible. In that regard it is somewhat similar to P12, the ten generation fan-shaped chart and the P3 listing eight generations.

The A2 Pedigree Chart is designed for the three-ring binder. It has spaces for the same number of ancestors as the P1 and the same arrangement to extend your pedigree to your most remote ancestor. It will fit into an ordinary typewriter -- all others fit only the wide carriage typewriters. The A24 has spaces for four generations.

## FORM LETTERS

Most researchers at some time or another have to write for information on a particular phase of their family line to some unknown individual. To many people letter writing is a difficult chore. They take too much time and space to express their need. Form P5 is designed to make such a task a most pleasant undertaking. On one side is a short printed letter asking for the needed information with spaces to insert a minimum of words. It has been written by an experienced letter writer using the modern idea that to get the best results, a letter requesting information must take the receiver's point of view rather than the writer's point of view. In other words it is a "you" letter rather than an "I" letter. If you don't care to send a "form letter" for information you might want to use it as a pattern for a personal letter.

On the same side as the letter is a three generation pedigree chart on which the sender notes the names and the relationship of the persons whose data is desired. On the opposite side of the sheet is a four generation pedigree chart to be completed by the receiver of the inquiry and returned to the sender. A lot of time and bother is saved by all concerned by use of this handy sheet. Remember, P5 may save you hours of correspondence!

If you would like more information on how and where to write for genealogical records and data, read the HANDBOOK FOR GENEALOGICAL CORRESPONDENCE, written by the staff of the Cache Genealogical library, published by Bookcraft, also THE HANDY BOOK FOR GENEALOGISTS, Published by the Everton Publishers. (see page 221)

## LISTING NAMES ON THE PEDIGREE CHARTS

When looking at a pedigree chart for the first time the genealogical novice may feel bewildered and uncertain how to proceed. It should be remembered, first of all, that a pedigree chart is a genealogical tree, a table presenting all known ancestors of person No. 1.    Brothers and sisters of one family may be listed in a group as No. 1 on chart No. 1, but all others listed must be parents, grandparents and great grandparents.  The name in the No. 1 space on the first chart may be your own, your spouse, your children, your brothers and sisters, your father or mother, or any one whose ancestry is to be traced.   If you take one or all of your children for No. 1, it will be your family group pedigree chart, the only one of its kind in the whole world, entirely different than all others.   It ties together your family and that of your spouse -- only you and your children can claim it.

Each person has the most important part of his or her identifying data, such as the full name, when and where born, when married, and when and where died.  As in the case of the Family Group Sheet, the married name of women should never appear on the pedigree chart -- always it should be the maiden surname. The abbreviation of names -- even the common ones such as Geo., Thos., Chas., etc. -- should be avoided on the pedigree and the Family Group Sheet.

It is well to indicate on the back of the pedigree chart where the data was obtained. Refer to names by their number. The father of No. 1 is placed on line No. 2; the mother of No. 1 on line No. 3. The father of No. 2 becomes No. 4, the mother No. 5. The father of No. 3 becomes No. 6, the mother No. 7. By following this pattern all males will have even numbers and all females odd numbers, with the exception of No. 1 which may be either male or female.

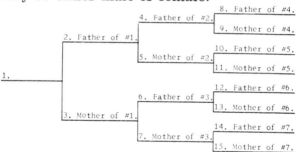

AN UNLIMITED PEDIGREE RECORD

As previously mentioned charts Nos. A2, P1 and P7 are designed to accommodate five generations which can be continued by using additional charts. In using this system, fill out your pedigree on any one line until you come to the fifth generation which is represented by Nos. 16 to 31, inclusive. Indicate in the space provided that the line is continued on chart Number Two. Take your next chart, mark it No. 2 and place the name of the above mentioned person in the No. 1 position. You will also find a space on this sheet which refers back to the previous chart. Fill in the needed information showing that this person (No. 1) is the same person as No. ____ on Chart No. 1 -- thus giving your reference directions backwards as well as forward. Continue on with the pedigree of the above person (No. 1 on Chart No. 2) as far as you can. When you again reach the fifth generation position on Chart No. 2, which of course, would be the ninth generation from the original No. 1, mark the next chart No. 3. Indicate in the proper places provided on the sheet that this person's pedigree is continued on Chart No. 3 and again make the back reference indicating that person's number on Chart No. 2. Continue this process as far as is necessary to record the information you have gathered on this direct ancestral line. You may then take another line on Chart No. 1 and follow it through in the same manner. It doesn't make much difference which ancestral line you trace first or the order in which they are traced so long as you indicate on each fifth generation name, the number of the sheet which continues that line and that your reference numbers on

each chart are correct.    The following
examples may help you to understand the
written directions.

Chart No. 1                              16. Aaron Brown
                                         Continued on Chart No. 4.


1. You - - - - - - - - -                 19. Mary Smith
                                         Continued on Chart No. 2.


                                         26. William White
                                         Continued on Chart No. 5.


* * * * * * * * * * * * * * * * * * * * * * * * * * * * * * * *


Chart No. 2
Person No. 1 on this chart is
the same person as No. 19
on Chart No. 1

1. Mary Smith - - - - - - - - 24. John Jones
                                         Continued on Chart No. 3.


* * * * * * * * * * * * * * * * * * * * * * * * * * * * * * * *


Chart No. 3
Person No. 1 on this chart is
the same person as No. 24
on chart No. 2

1. John Jones - - - - - - - -


* * * * * * * * * * * * * * * * * * * * * * * * * * * * * * * *


Chart No. 4
Person No. 1 on this chart is
the same person as No. 16
on Chart No. 1

1. Aaron Brown - - - - - - - 16. George Brown
                                         Continued on Chart No. 6.

Chart No. 5
Person No. 1 on this chart is
the same person as No. 26
on Chart No. 1

1. William White   - - - - - - - -

* * * * * * * * * * * * * * * * * * * * * * * * * * * * * * * *

Chart No. 6
Person No. 1 on this chart is
the same person as No. 16
on Chart No. 4

1. George Brown   - - - - - - - -

* * * * * * * * * * * * * * * * * * * * * * * * * * * * * * * *

By following this system you can add to
your pedigree as the information is gathered
-- some today, some tomorrow, and some
next year.   Pedigrees needing thirty or
forty sheets are not at all uncommon.
Occasionally some are found with one
hundred to several hundred sheets. However, no matter what size it is, it is an
easy matter to trace any family line
either backwards or forwards.   The important thing is to keep the charts in nu-
merical order and to be sure the reference
numbers are correct in both directions.

This method does not show at a glance
the whole pedigree as do some of the
specially drawn charts. But for permanent

records these are more easily handled and better protected in a substantial binder. Each chart has plenty of space with each name for identifying information on each person as to birth, marriage and death. Additional leaves may be added as the lines are extended. Chart forms A2,A24,P1 and/or P7 lay the foundation for any special pedigree chart you may wish to construct, and assist you in organizing your research campaign.

Under ordinary circumstances only blood lines should be followed on the pedigree chart. However if you do find foster parents on your lines and wish to trace their ancestry because it is impossible to connect to the blood line, clearly indicate on your chart that they are foster parents. Record the truth -- nothing else will stand the test of time.

As you become more acquainted with genealogical books and charts you will find some very complicated pedigree charts. Almost every one of these have been arranged in a special manner to show special connections. None of them show all the ancestors which might have been found as can be shown when using the above system. To make an explanation of the construction methods used to draw up these special pedigrees would take considerable space and would be of little value as each one would require special treatment and they are all different. Don't worry about them until you have to, if ever, then get an expert to help you if you can't figure them out for yourself. Simplicity and completeness are embodied in the system using Forms A2, A24, P1 and P7 more than in any other system we are acquainted with.

## FAMILY HISTORY SHEETS

Genealogy and history are closely connected. In many ways they complement and assist each other. In fact, it is difficult to separate them. Genealogists have learned it is well to keep a record of historical facts pertaining to family members. It enriches the family record, preserves notable family deeds, unites more firmly family members, freshens family traditions, assists in the identification of family members, and, above all, adds interest to the genealogical record.

Often, when in a meditative mood, you have chuckled inwardly as almost forgotten incidents have passed in review before your inner eyes. If they were known to

your children or children's children would-
n't they cause them to chuckle, too? And,
yet, when some one suggests to you that you
should write a history of your life, you shrug
your shoulders with the comment, "Oh,
nothing of importance ever happened to me.
My life is just a dreary repetition of unin-
teresting events." You better discard that
notion right now. If you don't use a typewriter, you better take your pen in hand
and write some of the things you can remember from your childhood and courtship days.
As you get started, you will be surprised
over the many incidents that come rushing
through your mind. Your pen can't keep up
with the onrushing memories of by-gone
days. If you have a son or daughter or
other relative acquainted with shorthand tell
your stories to one of them. It would be
better if the two of you were in a room alone,
where nothing can disturb or interfere with
you. In an hour you would have quite a bit
of fascinating history. You could repeat
that every day or so for a month or longer
and you would have a priceless history to
leave with your posterity.

If any member of your family has a recording machine, which are now in vogue,
you may merely tell your story to it. Before starting to dictate a record you should

make up a draft or an outline of the things you want to talk about.

Family History Sheets are available from most genealogical supply houses. S1 measures 8½x14, S2 and A3 8½x11, all are ruled and punched on a fifty percent rag bond twenty pound paper. It is a good practice to place the Family History Sheet following the Family Group Sheet -- then with the pictures facing the front of the Family Group Sheets and the history on the back, the record of one family is complete.

## SUGGESTIONS AND ITEMS TO CONSIDER IN WRITING YOUR PERSONAL HISTORY

1. Your birth: when, where, parents, surrounding circumstances and conditions.

2. Your childhood: health, diseases, accidents, playmates, trips, associations with your brothers and sisters, unusual happenings, visitors in your home, visits to grandparents, relatives you remember, religion in your home, financial condition of parents.

3. Your brothers and sisters: names, date of birth, place of birth, accomplishments, names of spouses, date and place of marriage, their children.

4. Your school days: schools attended, teachers, courses studied, special activities, associates, achievements, socials, report cards, humorous situations, who or what influenced you to take certain courses or do things you might not otherwise have done.

5. Your activities before, after and in between school sessions: vacations, jobs, attendance at church, other church functions, scouting, sports, tasks at home, fun and funny situations.

6. Your courtship and marriage: meeting your spouse, special dates, how the question was popped, marriage plans, the wedding, parties and receptions, gifts, honeymoon, meeting your in-laws, what influenced you most in your choice of spouse.

7. Settling down to married life: your new home, starting housekeeping, bride's biscuits, spats and adjustments, a growing love, making ends meet, joys and sorrows, your mother-in-law, other in-laws.

8. Your vocation: training for your job, promotions, companies you worked for,

salaries,, associates, achievements, your own business.

9.    Your children: names, dates and places of birth, health of mother before and after, how father fared, characteristics, habits, smart sayings and doings, growing up, accomplishments, schooling, marriage, vocations, sicknesses, accidents, operations.

10.   Your civic and political activities: positions held, services rendered, clubs, fraternities and lodges you have joined, military service record.

11.   Your church activities: as a young person, through adolescence, churches attended, church positions, church associates, church certificates, answers to prayers, necessity and power of love.

12.   Your avocations: sports, home hobbies, dramatic and musical activities, reading habits, genealogy, travels, favorite songs, movies, books, writers, poems, etc.

13.   Special celebrations or holidays you remember: Easter, Christmas, national and local holidays, vacations.

14. Your plans and hopes for the future.

15. Your ancestors: your impressions of those you knew personally; a general sketch of those you did not know; father, mother, grandparents, great grandparents, and other relatives.

16. Your encouragement and counsel to your descendants: carrying on family traditions and activities; their obligations to their country, church and family; your suggestions to your progeny and others on honesty, humility, health, diligence, perseverance, thrift, loyalty, kindness, reverence, the Bible and other religious and edifying books; service to fellowmen; your belief regarding God, etc.

Never underestimate the effect you may have on unborn generations in helping them through the trials and tribulations of life by the written word of advice you leave your children, grandchildren, etc. If you would like them to live upright honest lives, give them the benefit of your experiences. Job, of the Old Testament, lamented the fact that his words were not written when he said, ''Oh that my words were now written! Oh that they were printed in a

book!    That they were graven with an
iron pen and lead in the rock forever!"
(Job, 19-23)    But they were written,
and he then gave his beautiful testimony
of the Redeemer which has been used
countless times as the text of sermons
in both the Jewish and the Christian
worlds.    Your communications to your
descendants must be written.    They
will also appreciate your life story as a
precious treasure, and bless you all
their days for it.

Hints on writing your life story: tell
your story plainly and with directness;
write truthfully of uplifting, refined
and honorable occurrences and experiences.    Humor helps to make for easier
reading.    If you can give the whys of
your decisions and changes in activities
it may help others. Illustrate with as
many pictures as possible. Make several copies, or better still, mimeograph
or print and give one to each of your
children and grandchildren.    Place
copies in local and national libraries
and/or historical societies.

## ARRANGING AND UTILIZING YOUR RECORD FOR THE GREATEST SATISFACTION

Many advantages will be gained by using

loose leaf sheets and binder for the preservation of your valuable records. You can add to your book at will or re-arrange it as you may desire any time. You may find additional historical facts or discover some valuable pictures which you want to add to your collection. You can make such changes any time you desire. Additions to living families, new marriages or deaths can be added as they occur. The place for recording these events is the Family Group Sheet. The time for recording these events is immediately after they have occurred while it is still on your mind. "A stitch in time saves nine."

In putting your book together some order is necessary if you are to locate with ease the sheets you have compiled. Many have found it a good idea to place the pedigree sheets in the front of the book followed by their own family group pictures, record and history. After this they place the records of their married children, if any, and then the records of all ancestors and relatives in alphabetic order, using the husband's surname as a guide. If you find several husbands with the same surname, arrange them according to their age, the eldest first and so on. If a husband has had more than one wife, place wife No. 1 first, No. 2 second, and so on.

WHY A GENEALOGICAL RECORD?

It is a real honor to claim descent from pioneer ancestors. Many have traced their lines to progenitors who landed on the bleak shores of New England on November 20, 1620. Descendants of that brave band now belong to "Society of Mayflower Descendants." It was organized in December 1894 to preserve the memory, the records, the history, and all the facts relating to the "Mayflower" Pilgrims, their ancestors and their posterity. All lineal descendants of the original pilgrims are qualified for membership.

Many societies have grown out of the desire to honor the memory of those stalwarts who fought for the independence of our nation. "The National Society of the Daughters of the American Revolution," (DAR), and the "National Society of the Sons of the American Revolution," (SAR), two of the largest, have thousands of members proud of the part their ancestors played in the establishment of our beloved country.

All of the original colonies have similar societies, all of them dedicated to honoring the memory of the originators. Those desiring membership in these patriotic organizations must prove their eligibility with an authentic pedigree showing their descent from the claimed ancestors.

Your genealogical record will form the basis of the record necessary to join many of these organizations. You will be proud to prove that on your family tree are some who helped lay the foundation for this nation or performed other notable deeds worthy of unceasing praise.

## WRITE A HISTORY

Another use for the information you may gather and assemble in your genealogical record is as a basis for a printed book honoring the memory of your ancestors -- giving their history and recording their descendants. Recognizing a great truth, Daniel Webster said, "He who careth not from whence he came, careth little whither he goeth." Your vision will be focused on the future by seeking the records of and venerating those who gave you your heritage. You are looking ahead by looking back.

## MICROFILMING

It may be that you will not be prepared to

publish a book after your work of assembling your loose-leaf record, yet you recognize that something should be done to preserve it for generations to come. In such cases, you may find microfilming the solution to your problem. By this method your record can be put on a small roll of film at a small cost. If you take your record to a genealogical library they may be willing to make a copy for their own use at no cost at all to you. In most large cities are companies who make a business of microfilming. Look in the classified pages of the telephone book if you desire their services. A few microfilm copies placed strategically with genealogical libraries would assure the preservation of your records for all time.

But, what if you neither want it published or microfilmed? Well, the personal satisfaction of having compiled the record ordinarily compensates for all the time, effort and money expended in the pursuit of your family tree and the record of your relatives. It is a fascinating hobby, delving into history, geography, court records, church records -- on familiar ground as well as in foreign places. It has been reduced to a science and is now taught in many schools in many parts of the world. Once it is started, it is difficult to abandon. But it should be done right to derive the greatest pleasure. You will be on the right tract if you follow the instructions in this book. Practice will eventually lead to perfection.

## NOTES

# II

# How To Continue

Genealogy continues to attract more and more people as devotees of this extremely interesting pastime. Ancestral information is gathered every year with accelerating impetus. And with this growing activity of searchers comes an impulsion to record keepers, private and public, to assist by making more records available. Advanced printing and copying devices have also helped to make antecedent hunting much easier than in former times. Every year sees hundreds of new genealogy books and other printed aids in the hands of those who are desirous of extending their knowledge of their parental and collateral lines.

And, yet genealogy is not easy to find. It still requires lots of ingenuity and long hours and months of diligent study. But a sincere researcher never gets discouraged. Although it takes a lot of work, he knows success seldom comes without planned and applied effort. If one method fails, another is tried until the needed information is finally found.

The suggestions that follow should be read and reread time and again since it is dif-

ficult to retain everything read in one sitting.
One of the best memory systems is to tell
someone else what you have read. After you
have repeated it four or five times, it stays
with you. In other words, if you want to keep
anything, you must give it to others. The
oftener you give it away, the more it remains
with you.

## REGISTER YOUR RESEARCH ENDEAVORS

One of the difficulties genealogists find as
they proceed with their research endeavors
is that they make searches of certain records  and  make  no  notations of these
searches.  Then after a lapse of time they
forget what and where they have searched
and turn again to the same sources - dis-
tinctly a waste of time. To help eliminate
this trouble many of the serious researchers
have taken to making a log or register of all
their searches. Every time they engage in
any research activity they make a short record of it; the date; the name of the book or
record; a brief statement of results.

To assist those who desire to make such
a register. The Everton Publishers have
made available a form called ''Research
Register'', A5. It advises that you number
your searches as well as date them. Also

that you transfer the number of the search to the record you make of that search, such as the family group sheet, the form A4 (a description of which follows) or other record. Then if questions arise you may quickly refer from the register to your record or vice versa to check any point you wish. It may save you a lot of time later on if you make such a register of your quests for ancestor material.

In connection with your "register" you may also want to start a system of filing the old letters, birth, marriage and death certificates, copies of wills and other court records, etc., which you may gather as you glean forefather facts. A good system used by many is very simple. Just take a common 14 inch file folder and use prong fasteners to secure to the folder each certificate, old letter, photo copy or other piece of evidence you might gather. This is a system used by most lawyers and business firms to preserve valuable letters, etc. Supplies for this may be purchased at any office supply house. Number each piece consecutively as you fasten it in the folder and register that number on your A4 also on your permanent record to give you quick reference as to where it is filed if ever you need it for further study.

## SUGGESTIONS
## TO HELP SOLVE DISCREPANCIES

As you start recording the names, dates and places respecting your relatives and ancestors you will find that all records do not agree in the data they reveal. Dates may vary, names may be spelled differently, places and relationships may not correspond. This is extremely disconcerting to the beginner. To help to solve this difficulty you should first record word for word and letter for letter the information you find on each record, and state where you found the data. This can be easily accomplished by using Form A4 which has spaces provided for most catagories of facts used in genealogical records. It also has spaces for indicating various types of records making it possible for you to just check ✓ your source.

After you have searched all records available regarding this person you may lay out all your form A4's on him and easily make comparisons. In some cases you may want to use a ''Discrepancy Chart'', Form R3, and put all the information in question on one sheet to make it even more handy to compare and check.

Then comes the task of deciding which record is right and which is wrong. A good rule to follow, though it is not always true, is that the record that was made nearest to the date of the event is the one most likely to be correct. For instance, a date of birth from a Parish Record is much more likely to be right than one taken from a census record. Or, a marriage date taken from a marriage certificate undoubtedly would be more acceptable than one from a personal history written years after the event. A death date on a tombstone errected years later should not have the weight given an old letter written a few days after the death. The place of birth recorded in a biography would more than likely be erroneous if it disagreed with a birth certificate.

## NUMEROUS ERRORS

Just because you find an event written in a book or even in several books doesn't always make it a fact. Many an error has been copied and recopied over and over again. Printed records are excellent sources for clues but unless the author has documented his facts or has given references as to where he obtained his material, be careful, it may be that he has reproduced errors of others or made mistakes of his own. And though he has documented and referenced his book, it would still be well for you to test his sources to be sure he has not erred in his judgment or transcriptions.

Original, official records usually are the most reliable sources for genealogical information -- contemporary recordings in most cases would be considered next best -- then the records made after the event. But, this does not hold in all cases.

The official cemetery record of Isaac Gaisford gave 1875 as his birth date (he died in 1890), but all other unofficial records gave 1815 as his birth. As he had married twice before 1875, had immigrated to America in 1852, had 12 children, and had been recorded in other unofficial contemporary records long before 1875, that date had to be discarded for 1815. It can be easily seen how the seven could have been substituted by the recorder for the one to make this error.

Poor memories, mistakes in copying, as well as intentional deceptions have caused countless errors in records, making it necessary to check as many sources as possible and weigh all the evidence before making a decision as to which is right. Much more information can be found regarding evaluating records in Derick Harland's "Genealogical Research Standards" available at most genealogical supply houses.

## PROVE YOUR RECORDS

The satisfaction of a job well done comes only by doing the job at hand properly. If you want the most out of your genealogical activities use the methods which long experience has found to be the right methods. Avoid errors by correctly copying names, dates and places. Proof read carefully everything you have written. Prove all data and indicate how and where you have proved it.

In the past many researchers have failed because they have taken too many things for granted which later were proved wrong. Just because you read something in a book or a newspaper, don't take for granted that it is true. Prove it before you make it a permanent part of your record. And when you have proved it, show where the information was obtained, so others also may be sure of its correctness. The novice may say, "Well, all of that is easy to say, but how is it done?" A substantial portion of the expert genealogists use the legal method to prove their records -- they have photostatic or certified copies of birth, marriage and death certificates, wills, etc. to prove every step or point in their records. Some consider this is not necessary. They deem it sufficient to indicate where the information was obtained which is commonly called the historical method.

The large majority, however, probably use a combination of both methods, documenting their evidence where possible and citing their references otherwise. Choose which method you prefer but be sure you do not fail to indicate where or from whom you gained your information as you record it. If you don't, you may forget and then later on wish that you had noted your source. Using the A4 "Data Work Sheet" and the A5 "Research Register" will help if not entirely eliminate this difficulty of wondering where you obtained your data when you want to check it.

## LITTLE EQUIPMENT NEEDED

If you are just beginning your genealogical research activities, you don't need to load yourself down with a lot of equipment. All you need is a ten cent notebook or a few Form A4, Data Work Sheets (which may prove to be a valuable help in guiding you in what to seek or ask for and helping you to record your findings.) These you can carry in your coat pocket, or, if a woman, in your handbag with a few sharpened soft-lead pencils. If you use a mechanical pencil, it may be well, for the sake of insurance, to bring along an extra box of leads. If you are going to call on some relatives for whatever information you can pick up, you may take along a fountain pen, if you desire. But you should remember that most libraries prohibit the use of ink when copying from their books. If the pen leaks there is a chance some of the printed words may be completely obliterated. The most important part of your "equipment" is an inquisitive mind, a pleasant attitude, and a knack in asking questions.

## IT TAKES TIME TO FIND GENEALOGY

The suggestions offered here may help you find some of your ancestors. Again, they may bring you no results. No one can tell for sure where you can find genealogy. The best any one can do is to suggest where you may find it. If you hire a professional genealogist, he will search where he thinks your records are. Regardless how careful he may be, he will find nothing if your records are not there. No reliable genealogist ever guarantees to find any particular record unless he definitely knows it is there. Hence, you should not feel discouraged or cancel the search should you have the experience of paying for a search that brings no returns.

Likewise, you may write thousands of letters without results. Most of them may never be answered, the others have nothing to tell you. Many family events, such as marriages, births, and deaths were never recorded where we would expect them to be. If you fail to find them at once, don't quit, but try the harder. Undoubtedly they were recorded somewhere, and eventually you will find it, even if it should take years. By following the suggestions recorded here many people have found the desired results.

## ASK YOUR OWN FAMILY FIRST

It is not at all uncommon for the beginner in research activities to spend time and money in genealogical pursuits only to find that other members of the family have already searched and found the same names. To avoid such unnecessary waste of time and means always start your research in your own family. Here are some questions to which you should have the answers before going too far into your research.

1. Is some other family member searching for genealogy on your branch of the

family?

2. What family member has more genealogical data than you have?

3. Does any branch of the family own an
   old family Bible containing any genealogical information?

4. Does any family member have in his
   possession copies of gravestone inscrip-
   tions in old, forgotten family grounds?

If yours is a large family scattered over
many states, it may require many letters
and more months to get the needed information.  Besides uncles and aunts, you should
write to cousins of the third, fourth, and
fifth degree, as well as first and second
cousins, and in-laws who may have records
and information of some of your dead relatives.

"Ten Basic Steps in Genealogy" published by the Genealogical Society of the
Latter-Day Saints Church lists 8 points
to consider when you write a letter.

1. Letters should be CLEAN and ATTRAC-
   TIVE in appearance.  Don't write in
   pencil or with red, green, or purple ink.
   A typewritten letter or one written clearly and legibly in black or blue-black ink
   on a clean sheet of paper will go a long

way in creating a good first impression.

2.  BE COURTEOUS! Don't demand information. Ask for the assistance of the person to whom you are writing. Enclose a stamped, addressed envelope for the reply.

3.  BE CLEAR! If the reader doesn't fully understand what you want, he can't possibly send it to you. Don't leave what you want to the imagination of the recipient. Ask for what you want in plain language.

4.  BE CONCISE! Don't assume that the reader will ''plough'' through page after page searching for one request item. Be brief!

5.  BE HELPFUL! Make your letter easy to read and easy to answer. If you are asking for several items, number your requests 1, 2, 3, etc. Itemizing your requests will make your letter easier to answer.

6.  BE REASONABLE--DON'T ASK FOR TOO MUCH AT ONE TIME! Don't expect persons who have been active in genealogical work for years to send you a copy of all the pedigree charts and family group records in their possession. To satisfy such a request could involve weeks, even months of copying, and so offer to do any copying involved.

7. OFFER TO SHARE WHAT GENEALOG-
   CAL INFORMATION YOU HAVE! If a
   relative is aware that you will pass on
   what information you have there is a
   better chance of his sharing with you.
8. PLAN YOUR LETTER CAREFULLY!
   Write an outline first, then a rough
   draft. Next go over it item by item before preparing the final letter.

Letters reveal your character, your per-
sonality, just as does your face and actions.
Since you desire to make a good impression
on the persons from whom you are seeking
family information, you should be careful
that the looks and the tone of your letter
represent you precisely as you would want
to present yourself personally to these individuals.

While we should remember that genealogical letters are not particularly love
letters, it is nevertheless not amiss when
writing to recall the effusion of Ella Wheel-
er Wilcox in her beautiful poetical story,
"Maurine":

"Letters all blots, though finely written,
   show
A slovenly person. Letters stiff and white
Bespeak a nature honest, plain, upright.

And tissuey, tinted, perfumed notes, like
   this,
Tell of a creature formed to pet and kiss."

## PERSONAL VISITS ARE BEST

Letter writing is a good way for you to gain the needed information, but personal visits are far better. Most people would rather talk than write. That's why thousands of letters go unanswered. If your grandparents or other older members of your family, like brothers or sisters of any of your grandparents, live even two or three hundred miles away, it would pay you in the long run, to visit with them.

Many experienced researchers spend their vacation periods doing research work in the community where their grandparents or great grandparents lived. They visit not only with relatives but with former neighbors or intimate associates of their ancestors, most of whom generally have something worthwhile to add to the data desired. On-the-spot research generally is productive of a wealth of information.

To be a successful genealogist you must be a willing listener. You must train yourself to ask short, direct questions, and then listen intently to the, perhaps, long drawn-out story of the interviewed relative. Be careful that you never offend or injure the feelings of the person questioned. Never mention anything to him that may be repulsive to him. On the contrary, do everything possible to gain his friendship, good will and confidence. Remember that you are trying to get from him family information unknown to you. Until you get that, let your conversation with him be strictly genealogical.

Keep your notebook handy while he is talking with you. As you listen, carefully select from his story the points of value and interest you need for your records. Write them in your notebook while he is talking. If dates and names are given, be sure to write them correctly, being careful to get the right spelling of names and places. Don't take anything for granted. Whenever you're in doubt, ask questions and record the answers.

If he has any old family Bibles or records, ask permission to see them. Copy from them whatever valuable family information they may contain. Record the births, marriages, deaths, etc. Also the date the Bible was printed and whether the writing in it appears to have been recorded all at one time or at different times, such as, near the time of each event. Old Bible information is wonderful but it is much more acceptable if the record is contemporary with the occurence. So it is with all other records -- the greater the lapse of time between the event and the recording of the event the greater the chance of error.

Don't be satisfied with information received from one relative or a single source. Contact other family members and relatives and compare the information they give you with what you have already gathered. Never discard any information until you are sure it is wrong. "Genealogical Research Standards" by Dereck Harland will assist you in evaluating your records. It is also an excellent book to assist you to save time in your research by showing you how to organize and proceed to solve your problems.

Sometime it may happen that the interviewed person seems loath to discuss some member of the family. You may feel he is hedging or hiding things from you -- that he wants to cover up things rather than to bare them. Assure him quickly that you are not particularly interested in any "skeletons-in-the-closet," that nothing like that will be mentioned or revealed by you in your records, but that you are primarily interested in getting the statistical information about the individual -- birth, marriage and death dates, and other pertinent facts about the family in question.

## PROVE FAMILY TRADITIONS

Tradition is a statement, opinion or belief, or a body of statements or opinions or beliefs, that has been handed down from age to age by oral communication, without the aid of written memorials. Many families have traditions that have come down from earlier days. In olden times there were no movies, no theaters, no radio, no television. During the long, dark nights of those years, the family gathered around the fireplace watching the burning logs. Older family members told and retold stories about the family ancestors and their accomplishments. Those stories grew with each telling and eventually developed into traditions to which the family has clung as valuable mementos. Some of these traditions are true. Others are based on inaccuracies and the more vivid imaginations of the story tellers.

Never embrace any family tradition with too much enthusiasm. Search, investigate

and prove every pretended relationship
with men of high estate -- statesmen,
barons, nobles or royal family members.
Carefully trace the tradition to its origin
and it may appear more drab and common
place than it did after years and years of
industrious applications of an imaginary
lustrous tint, continuously polished by an
over-inflated ego. However, if the tradition
is founded on fact, you may be able to extend
that particular family line on your pedigree
chart for several generations since such
families have usually maintained printed
genealogies for many centuries.

## PEDIGREES MUST BE CORRECT

An accurate genealogy is priceless. Diligence is the price paid for accuracy. All
source material must be thoroughly searched and weeded. If the remaining material
is complete it can be woven into an accurate
family record.    Just to scan the source
material will not insure an accurate record.

Accuracy is of prime importance. Even
though it may take a longer time, it will
bring a lasting satisfaction. By employing
all available sources of information errors
can be eliminated and the work done well.

Every pedigree delineation must be based
on facts.  One little mistake may invalidate

months of research on a wrong line. Too often tradition is built on misinformation and false hearsay. Let us caution you again to check carefully all rumors or traditions before you start to incorporate them into your pedigree. Some people have the false notion that anything appearing in print is correct. The person who prepared the material for printing may have built the article on a wrong premise. If he were correct, the typesetter or the proofreader may have made an error. While reporters and newspaper workers don't make mistakes deliberately, sometimes they may be careless. In checking an obituary in an old newspaper, we found three glaring mistakes in one name. That's poor proofreading!

We have seen beginners in research extend an already started pedigree. They failed to check on the accuracy of the data given. They were unaware of the fact that the person who had started the chart had jumped at conclusions and had entered names and other data entirely foreign to that pedigree. Naturally all of that work was worthless and had to be discarded. Several months of hard work had to be eliminated.

## MANY PEOPLE - SAME NAME

There are thousands of persons with

exactly the same name. In checking a name file in a genealogical library, we found nine hundred different individuals bearing the name of Nils Rasmusson, all of them born at different times and different localities in Sweden. In one community we knew two men bearing the name of William West. One of them lived in the east part of town, the other in the west. To distinguish them the townspeople called one of them William East. But fifty years from now if the researchers are looking for them they will find both of them on the records as William West.

A woman in an adjoining state wrote us to help her find one of her husband's ancestors by the name of Christopher Black who came from Germany to Maryland before the Revolutionary War. In reading her letter we said to ourself, "There never was a man coming out of Germany with the name of Black." We checked several early records but were unable to find a Christopher Black. When we followed our first hunch on reading the letter, we found a Christopher Schwartz who had been named an Ensign in the armed forces supplied by Maryland for the war.

There are in America many Nelson families who originated in Sweden. Should you look for them in Sweden remember that the name is Nilsson. Many Families coming from various countries of Europe have Americanized their names after being here for a while. Be sure to take that into consideration when you are looking for your ancestors in their original habitat. Many of these foreign descendants know little or nothing about their mother tongue. They have only their names, perhaps wholly or partially anglicized, to remind them that their background is different from that of their neighbors.

Also, be sure to consider the possibility of a different spelling of any name if you have difficulty in extending your lines. Prior to the 20th century comparatively few people could spell their own names. They had to rely on the priest, the clerk of the court, the tax collector or other recorders to do the spelling for them. It is not unusual to find one person with the records of the church spelling his name one way, the court another way, the census another way and the vital statistics still another way. He pronounced his name to the recorder in each case -- the recorder wrote it as it sounded to him. If the recorder had English training he wrote it the English way. If he was of French origin he brought the French influence into the spelling. In one case a family had been known by the name of DeMille for several generations in Dutchess County, New York. They moved to New Jersey and the pastor of the Reformed Dutch Church recorded their names as Vandermilt, reverting to the Dutch custom. And so it is with practically every name -- you don't have to go very far back to find it spelled differently -- sometimes entirely different.

It would be well for you to record on your Form A4, or other note book, the various spellings of a name exactly as you find them. Then when you make up your Family Group Record use the earliest spelling as the main spelling but place the other spellings in parenthesis following the name to assist in further research problems.

As you add names to your pedigree, identify them with the names of the places in which they were born and died, also the dates of birth, marriage and death. If your Family Group Sheets are complete, this should be an easy matter. (See pages 5, 120)

SPELL PLACE NAMES CORRECTLY

Most obituaries of foreign born persons printed in American newspapers contain wrong or misspelled place names. The reason, in most cases, is about like this: Grandma came from Europe before her teens. She could talk her native language, but couldn't spell. If and when anyone wanted to make a record of her birthplace, it was written as it sounded to the American-trained ears of the writer when Grandma pronounced it. In most cases it was misspelled. Sometimes the spelling is so corrupt it is impossible to find the correct interpretation. The correct spelling of place names are of tremendous importance. Gazetteers are very useful in this connection. If your library does not have those you need, you may be able to have them get the ones you want from a lending library.

Another way to help untangle twisted up place names is to contact natives of those countries. Every American city has residents from almost every nation. Go to one of those born in Grandma's country and have him help you determine the correct spelling of her birthplace. They will feel honored you came to them for the assistance.

Some American-born children of European parents have the erroneous idea that more dignity comes to the family if their ancestors came from the capital of their native land. And so, when the birthplace is unknown to them, they sometimes add in explanation, "It was near Oslo, or Berlin, or Stockholm, or Amsterdam, or Copenhagen, or London, or Paris, or Bern." And this, even though the place may be hundreds of miles from the Capital. It muddles instead of clarifies the situation.

Let us repeat to emphisize a serious situation. Many Pedigree charts contain incorrect place names. Some of these errors come from faulty spelling. Ridiculous mistakes occur when names are spelled as pronounced, and often the pronunciation is entirely wrong. This is true not only in case of foreign place names but of American place names also. In other cases carelessly written records have been miscopied time and again. Sometimes the names of an estate, farm or of little neighborboods are given which are neither post offices nor churches. The post office name may be right, but it may be connected with the wrong county or state. It even occurs that names of rivers, canyons or lakes are given instead of the post office or parish. In most of the European countries are towns and localities in thirty or forty different parts of the particular country which bear exactly the same name. For that reason it is necessary that the name of the particular county accompanies the name of the locality. The same holds true in the United States. For instance, there is a Glenwood in at least twenty states in the union. Most of us know that Maine and Oregon each have a Portland, but how many know there are Portlands in fourteen other states. The same holds true with every nation in the world, no doubt. To differentiate between them we must have the town or city, the county, and the state or country. Otherwise you would not be able to pursue your genealogical research correctly. You may be able in each of those counties to find families of your surname, but it is doubtful if any of them but those in the correct county or nearby counties would belong to your ancestors.

Since these designations, town and county, are different in the various languages, we present herewith a list of them to make your research work lighter:

| State or Country | County | Town or City |
|---|---|---|
| Denmark | amt | by or stad |
| England | shire or county | borough or city |
| Finland | laani | kyla, kauppala or kaupunki |
| France | departement | village or ville |
| Germany | kreis | ort, dorf, or stadt |
| Iceland | sysla | sokn, baer |
| Ireland | shire | borough, city |
| Netherlands | provincie | dorp, stad |

| Norway | amt or fylker | by, sogn, stad |
| Scotland | shire | registration branch or city |
| Sweden | lan | by, koping, stad |
| Switzerland | bezirk, kanton | dorf, stadt |
| Wales | swydd | pentre, terf, dinas |

Be extremely careful that your pedigree chart is correct. If the personal names are known but the place names are unknown or wrong, it is impossible to do effective research. When errors are located in your record, be sure to correct all copies, so that the old error will not be recopied.

The dates should also approximate those belonging to other individuals in the similar brackets on the chart. That is to say, there should not be too great a variance in the birth and the marriage dates of the four grandparents, the eight great grandparents, etc. For instance, one pedigree chart we checked recently showed the greatest variance between the four grandparents to be twenty-seven years, between the eight great grandparents twenty-nine years, between the sixteen second great grandparents thirty years, between the thirty-two third great grandparents forty-nine years. Generally the ancestors on your father's side are older than those of your mother.

Other mistakes commonly found in genealogical records which have not been carefully checked include the following: death record prior to marriage or birth of a child; marriage date within a few years of birth date; marriage dates of two wives (or husbands) not consistent; children's birth dates not conforming with age of mother; children's birth dates too close; father's military record too early or late in life; and the like. Too much spread between the ages of husband and wife should also be checked very closely -- it may be correct but it is unusual. It is a wise proceedure to examine all dates and compare them with the rest of your record to see that they are all consistent and reasonable. If they are not, find out why.

## PROVE ALL WORK BEFORE CONTINUING

You can't be reminded too often that should you extend an already started pedigree chart, first be sure to prove the work done. Before you extend such a chart, you should be able to answer two questions: "Who placed this name on the chart?" and "How did he know it is correct?"

The same is true with most other records which may come into your hands. If possible have legal proof - evidence that will stand up in court - for every step up your ancestral ladder. This is not always possible, but, you should make it a rule to try every avenue to legally prove every name, date and relationship on your chart. Then you will be a real genealogist.

## DESIRED QUALITIES IN A RESEARCHER

Donald L. Jacobus, one of America's foremost genealogists, in his highly instructive book, "Genealogy as Pastime and Profession," says, "The genealogist should possess certain natural aptitudes, sharpened by experience, He should be painstaking, thorough, and accurate. He should be able to weigh evidence; to assemble in logical order a host of details; to construct hypotheses and test them. He needs the detective instinct, and experience must have taught him which of several clues is most likely to lead him to his object. He needs imagination, toned down by long training, and directed by sound reasoning. Especially he needs an excellent memory. Granted this natural equipment, much study and special knowledge are essential.

"A genealogist should not be opinionated, but should always keep on open mind and be ready to admit, on occasion, that his first conclusion was a mistaken one. Those who fear that admission of error will damage

their professional reputations as genealogists will not suffer much from any admission. Adherence to truth is more important than professional pride.''

## YOU MUST WRITE LETTERS

Making personal visits in search of your
genealogical data is undoubtedly the best
method, but also the most expensive. Some
letters must be written eventually to bring
together the needed information. Whether
you live in a remote part of a desolate
country section or adjacent to the largest
library in a populous city, letter writing
brings good returns to the researcher. Not
many people are inclined to letter writing.
It is a chore they hesitate to undertake and
therefore put it off as long as they can.
That is the reason so many of the letters
you send out go unanswered.

In writing your letters never mention anything about religion or politics. That may
stir up a hornet's nest. Hundreds of thousands of American families today are gene-
alogically minded. Hence it is absolutely
unnecessary for you to tell why you are
compiling your genealogy. Nobody particularly cares whether you are doing it as
a hobby, that you are writing a family

history, or that you want to leave with your children a knowledge of their heritage. You are gathering your genealogy - compiling your family tree - that is sufficient.

Unless you are writing to an intimate friend, don't write long, drawn-out letters - at least not the first ones you write to anybody. Make them brief, but to the point. State briefly and clearly what you are looking for. Give enough information as to names, dates and places to put the recipiant on the right track. One of the easiest ways to explain relationships is to send a short completed pedigree chart, showing the particular individuals involved in your inquiry.

You will save a lot of time and effort when writing for information if you use our Pedigree Chart No. P5. One side of that chart contains a short pedigree form and a printed letter asking for information. The pedigree form is a three generation chart. If you are asking for information on your paternal side, you need only to fill in the upper blanks of the chart; if on the maternal side, only the bottom section of the chart. The printed letter contains a blank space for you to fill in the name of the family you are seeking. The opposite side of the chart contains a four-generation pedigree chart which the recipient of your letter can fill in with the requested information. On this side also is a space for you to fill in the name and address of the person you are writing to. It is in such a position that the letter can be folded to fit a window envelope, thus avoiding the necessity of writing his name twice yet assuring you that his name will be on the sheet when it is returned.

Don't ask too many questions in your first letter. In subsequent letters, after relationship has been established, you may write more fully and more intimately. Then you may arrange your questions so that each one has a space following it for insertion of the answer. Always make it convenient for your correspondent to answer your questions with the least effort and in the shortest time possible. Courtesy demands that you enclose in your letter a stamped, self-addressed envelope unless you are writing to a public official or other person who is granted funds for such supplies. You should always offer to pay for any expense which might be incurred by the person gathering and compiling the information you want.

Be considerate in your requests. Don't ask for the sun, moon and the stars. Nobody will ever send them to you! One woman just starting out on her genealogical research wrote a man to send her "all the records you have on the So-and-So family." With a chuckle he tossed the letter in his yawning waste basket, while he removed the stamp from the self-addressed envelope that had been enclosed with the letter. He deemed the request unworthy of any kind of a reply. For more than thirty years he had been gathering information on the So-and-So family until at that time his records were bulging with almost twenty thousand individual names and the necessary data pertaining to them.

Had she been conservative and asked for information about one particular individual, it would have been sent to her gladly. Her letter revealed to him that she knew absolutely nothing about genealogical activities.

Sometimes your letters will go unanswered though you have used all the proper methods and your requests have been within reason. It is our opinion that many of these letters are not answered because the person who received them just didn't have the information to help you. At least let us hope this is the case.

Someone has said that the best way to get people to treat you nice is for you to treat them nice. Some researchers have had good success by sending a little gift in the letter, a handkerchief for a lady, etc. One man had some relatives in England who ignored his letters completely. He sent them a few cans of peaches during the war years. They didn't ignore him any more.

## CONTACT PERSONS OF SIMILAR NAMES

When searching for your family genealogy, you should never overlook any opportunity to contact people who may give you valuable information. In every large city in the nation are persons with the same surname as yours. Some of them may be distant relatives of yours. In starting your relative hunt a short pleasant note identifying yourself by naming your father, grandfather, and great grandfather, generally will bring some answers in the self-addressed envelope you enclosed in your letter. If there is no relationship, they may refer you to someone elsewhere who may be a relative. Or they may tell you of some one in their family who is compiling a family genealogy.

But how are you to find these people of your surname? Nothing difficult about that at all. Most libraries now days have in their files city directories and telephone directories from various parts of the country. If they haven't, you may have access to telephone directories in your local telephone office. At the office of your Chamber of Commerce, you may find city directories from many other cities.

## A MAGAZINE TO HELP YOU

The Genealogical Helper, a quarterly magazine, founded in 1947 has aided thousands of people all over the world. It is dedicated to helping more people find more genealogy. It is not confined to any particular section of the country but serves people in every state and many foreign countries. It is edited and published by the same concern publishing this book, The Everton Publishers Inc., HPO Box 368, Logan, Utah, 84321.

Three of the four yearly issues contain not less than forty pages, eight-and-a half by eleven inches. The September issues contain a hundred to two hundred or more pages and are called The Annual Exchange Editions. Each March issue contains a listing of family associations in the U.S. with the name and address of the person to write to regarding their genealogical interests.

The June issue contains the addresses of Genealogical Societies and Libraries, also professional genealogists, in the various states. In each March, June and December issue is a ''Question Box.'' About one hundred researchers ask for information in each issue on about two hundred fifty or three hundred different families on which they are working.

The first Annual Exchange Edition of ''The Genealogical Helper'' was published in 1950. Every year since then it has gained in popularity as thousands have found it pays to let the genealogical world know of their ancestor enigmas through its columns. Over the years there have probably been between thirty and forty thousand people who have ''registered'' their wants in the various Annual Exchange Editions. Many have sent unsolicited testimonials of how they have received the answers they wanted through someone reading their notice and volunteering the information. Other thousands have benefited by contacting those who have placed their names in the ''Helper.'' If you are interested send to the Everton Publishers, HPO Box 368, Logan, Utah, 84321, for a free catalogue which also lists many other genealogical aids.

## WHERE  TO  WRITE  FOR  GENEALOGY

A lot of personal and family information is available if we only knew where to go to find it.  Although it takes a longer time, it is cheaper to write for that information unless you live in proximity to the old family home.  Before addressing your envelopes, make out a list of the persons and organizations to which you intend to write.  List the name and the complete address of each. After you are through with the list place it in your genealogical file with a copy of your letter so you can find it any time you desire to check it.  When writing to strangers or organizations, it is always best to enclose a stamped self-addressed envelope for the expected reply.  Don't be irritated if we remind you of that courtesy too often - we believe it is for your best interests.  The following list is only suggestive.  You may think of many more.

Relatives, all kinds, everywhere.
Friends of the family, all dates.
Residents and former neighbors of the old home town.
Postmaster of the above, to locate relatives.
Names found in newspapers.
Names from directories.

City recorders, to locate records.

County judges, or county clerks, about marriage bonds or licences.

Family genealogists on your surname.

Genealogists living near the old home town.

Genealogical book stores for family and county histories.

Genealogists who search census records.

National Archives for early census.

Quaker researchers.

Immigration Bureau for arrivals.

Persons of your surname.

Genealogical libraries.

Bureau of Vital Statistics, each state capitol.

Newspapers for classified advertisements and old obituary notices.

LDS Church Historian's Office, Salt Lake City, Utah.

Rectors of English parishes.

Genealogists searching Great Britain Census.

Dominion Archives for Canadian census.

"Letters to the Editor" or forums of newspapers to locate unknown friends or relatives of the old home town.

## WRITING TO PUBLIC OFFICERS

No uniform method of record keeping is used by town and county offices. Some have cemetery or burial records that began many years ago. Some have birth records. Others have printed records of births, marriages and deaths, as well as other valuable information about the early settlers of the community. In each case it would be well to write the city recorder and ask for the information you want. If he does not have the records you want, he will direct you where to write.

The same is true of the county records. Various counties have used different methods of record keeping. Many counties throughout the United States have printed county histories with a lot of genealogy. Some have good records of wills and deeds and civil court actions. From all of these a great deal of genealogical information can be culled. If you find they have wills or other records pertaining to your family, a photostat copy will cost very little. A letter to the county clerk or the clerk of the court will bring from him the information you desire. Also if you find a book with a page or two of data you would like to have for your own, photostats of these may also be made.

Much more information on writing to public officials and others may be found

in HANDBOOK FOR GENEALOGICAL COR-
RESPONDENCE and THE HANDY BOOK
FOR GENEALOGISTS.  Both may be purchased from the Everton Publishers. (See
page 221)


## USE LABOR SAVING DEVICES

Sometimes you have to write to many
people to locate a lost relative. It takes a lot
of time and effort to write the same kind
of a letter to fifty or a hundred persons.  It
will be easier on your nerves to have the
letter mimeographed.  If you have a typewriter you can cut the stencil yourself,
thus cutting the cost materially.  Almost
every county seat or High School will have
a typewriter service equipped with mimeograph material. In that way you can cut the
cost of your letters down to a cent or two
each.   In some cases it may pay you to
include a pedigree chart to give the recipient a better idea of your family connections.
We again refer you to the P5 pedigree
chart mentioned in the previous chapter --
it will save a lot of labor, will clearly state
your wants and make it easy for your cor-
respondents to answer.  Possibly you can
make up you own letter and chart to serve
your purposes even better.

## FAMILY GENEALOGISTS

There are no more willing cooperators in this work than the family genealogists. They are active in this pursuit for the same reason that you are working in it. The easiest way to learn of them and their addresses is to secure a copy of one of the Annual Exchange Editions of THE GENEALOGICAL HELPER. Many libraries in the nation are subscribers to that magazine. If they are not, suggest to them to subscribe to it now, or you can send for a copy yourself. Remember, also, each March issue of the ''Helper'' since 1956 has had a list of family organizations.

You may greatly enrich your records by writing to all those compiling data on the families shown on your pedigree chart. This is especially true if their family and your family, the original families, lived in the same state. Like you, those people are compiling their own family genealogy, and they have access to information not printed in any book.

## HOME TOWN GENEALOGISTS

A genealogist living where your ancestors resided generally has access to records un-

known to you.  He is undoubtedly a member of a county historical society which has spent years in collecting data on the early inhabitants of the county.  He has access to birth and marriage records, death and cemetary records.

Sometimes you may get a lot of information for nothing.  However, you should remember that it takes a lot of time to search the records.  If you get a letter telling you of the available material but that it will cost you a certain amount of money for the time involved, accept the offer, if you can afford to pay for it, and it seems reasonable.

Family genealogists oft times have had limited experience in research.  Generally they have been concerned with the records of one family only.  Like the carpenter who has built only one house, they lack experience.  Learning to be a good genealogist is like learning to be a carpenter or a lawyer.  You can't learn it in a few easy lessons in a few weeks or months.  It takes time and effort and perserverance.  Years of practice, diligent application, will make you proficient, if you have the capacity to learn.

Most researchers occasionally find a knotty problem which stumps them.  The quickest way to get it solved may be to engage the services of an expert. A professional genealogist, one who has spent years in research, who has searched for many family lines in many places and who is a specialist in the genealogy of one particular part of the country or of one special kind of records, often can solve a hard problem quickly because he knows just where and how to look. Each June issue of THE GENEALOGICAL HELPER has a list of professional genealogists. If you desire the services offered by them you should check their qualifications and fields of research in the latest issue.

Time has been a great aid to the researcher. What years ago appeared as an insurmountable problem can often be solved easily today. Thousands of old records hidden away in unknown places have been discovered. They have been indexed and made easily available to the researcher. They have cleared up many problems that previously baffled the searcher. Every year sees hundreds of these lost records coming to light.

## WRITE TO GENEALOGICAL LIBRARIES

Good results have been obtained from writing to genealogical libraries. The li-

brarian knows what is in the library. With a minimum of effort she can find the data wanted. If you send a stamped envelope you will receive a courteous reply in most cases. Past experience indicates most librarians will attempt to find the information you are seeking, if it does not entail too much searching.

Information regarding residents of their home county is a specialty with most libraries. For that reason it may be well to write the library in the state and county where your people lived. Many times the small local libraries have information not obtainable in the larger libraries. Again the June issue of THE GENEALOGICAL HELPER will help you as it also lists libraries and Genealogical Societies of each state.

When you write to a library do not send a list of names. Ask about the ancestry of just one man or a man and his wife. Make identification easy by giving names of persons desired and whatever identifying information you have about them.

## PRINTED FAMILY HISTORIES

The easiest way to find genealogy is to find a printed book that gives the results of research done by others. Men some time spend a lifetime and a small fortune in searching for their family history and getting it printed in book form. When it is printed you can buy the book for five or ten dollars, even though thousands of dollars have been expended to get it printed. You may even be able to borrow it from the library. When you find a book, however, be sure to verify every step you may find in it that pertains to your direct ancestors.

During the past fifty years or more thousands of people have become interested in genealogy. Doctors, lawyers, educators, workmen in various fields, housewives, and office workers, in fact, people in all walks of life have suddenly become interested in searching for their ancestors. The desire to find out something about their progenitors seems to have struck them all at once. Enthusiastically they have searched among family relics, histories and official records. They have gathered information tirelessly for twenty or thirty years or more to satisfy the urge that has constantly been with them, spurring them on in their efforts to locate every source of information possible. Many of them have expended many thousands of dollars to secure their records. Generally few of them become satisfied with their

work until they have produced a printed volume for the safe keeping of their hard-earned history.

With the invention of new printing methods these family records can now be produced to fit almost any purse - they can be mimeographed, lithographed or letter-press printed.

One of the neatest and most interesting we have seen was also the easiest understood. It was the work of an architect and was built around our Pedigree Chart No. P8 and Family Group Sheet No. F2. Each sheet was first typewritten. Interspersed among these sheets were plain bond sheets, S5, on which were typewritten family and personal histories about the individuals mentioned on the preceding charts. This matter was typewritten in two four-inch columns on each sheet. The families were arranged and mentioned in the following order: The author, his wife and their children, his parents and their children, his grandparents and their children, his great grandparents and their children, his great great grandparents and their children, etc., etc. Picture pages were also included.

If the wife's family is to be included that

can be done following the completion of the husband's family in the same manner.

Other family histories begin with the oldest known progenitor and come down step by step to the present. In some cases each individual mentioned has been ingeneously numbered. For instance, if the first progenitor known is numbered 1, his first child, regardless of sex, becomes 11, the second 12, the third 13, etc. If someone is of the tenth or eleventh generation, the number may be one such as this: 1253-10-264. Let us explain this numbering: No. 1 is the original ancestor thus far known; the figure 2 indicates the second child of No. 1; the figure 5 indicates the fifth child of the preceding No. 2; the figure 3 indicates the third child of the preceding No. 5; the number 10 indicates the tenth child of the preceding No. 3 (only numbers above ten are hyphenated); the following No. 2 indicates the second child of the preceding No. 10 and so on. Only the direct descendants in the family are numbered. Wives and husbands of the direct descendants are mentioned only, not numbered. With this method, no two descendants of the same individual can have exactly the same number. Many other ways of numbering genealogical works have been devised. You may be able to figure out a system that will suit your particular record better than the above or any other used heretofore.

## LIBRARY CATALOGUES

More and more libraries are printing catalogues of the books they have in their various departments. The names of family histories and their authors are always included. If such catalogues are not available it is sometimes possible to learn from the librarian of any of the libraries in or near the locality of your early families whether or not histories of those families are available. If they refuse to let you borrow the book you may be able to hire some one there to check it for you to determine if any of your relatives are included. By getting the name and address of the publisher of the book you may be able to purchase a copy, or gain access to one.

It often costs less to buy a genealogical book than to hire someone to copy the information you need. It is always more satisfactory to own a book than to borrow it, if it contains much information for you. Today there are more family histories than ever before. Because only a limited number of copies of such histories are printed, the cost is much higher than the popular novel which are printed by the tens or hundreds of thousands. A genealogical book that looks like a dollar book may sell for $5.00 or more. Still, if you can buy a book for $5.00 you cannot afford to pay for getting it copied.

If you live in or near a large city, it will always pay you to spend several hours in a second-hand book store once in a while. Brouse around, thumb through book after book to get the general idea of their contents. Some time you'll find something that is just exactly what you want. Do the same thing in libraries you visit

BORROWING GENEALOGICAL BOOKS

One of the privileges that comes with joining some genealogical societies is that of borrowing books from their library even if you live thousands of miles from it. The annual dues generally are around $15. Besides that you have to pay the postage both ways on the books you borrow. If you are interested write to the society for information as to costs, etc. One of the foremost of these societies is the New England Historic Genealogical Society, 101 Newbury Street, Boston, Mass. 02116. The dues entitle you to the magazine published quarterly. The society owns one of the largest genealogical libraries in the United States.

If you join some of the patriotic socities, such as the Sons of the American Revolution, or the Daughters of the American Revolution you may also have access to information they have gathered over a hundred years or more.

Sometimes libraries in smaller cities are able to borrow books from the state library or other large institutions. Contact your librarian and ask her to help you get what you would like to obtain. Always treat her with courtesy and consideration and she may help you in ways unknown to you.

## RECORDS IN NATIONAL ARCHIVES

WAR RECORDS. Every state in the union which furnished soldiers for the Revolutionary War has histories containing the names of these men, and the branch of the service in which they were enlisted. In 1818 Congress passed an act establishing the first service pension law in the United States and provided pensions for all who had served at least nine months and were in indigent circumstances. In 1820 the War Department published the names of those who had applied for this pension. They were listed according to the states in which the enlistment was made. In 1955 the Genealogical Book Co., 521-23 St. Paul Place, Baltimore 2, Md. reprinted this valuable list containing more than 17,000 names. If one or more of your early American ancestors participated in the Revolutionary War and later received a pension, the names should be in that book. The names from each state are arranged in alphabetic order, making it easy to find the names in which you are interested. If they did not apply for a pension you may be able to find the names in the rosters published by the various states.

More often than not, the applications of these soldiers contain a lot of valuable genealogical information. Sometimes it pays the researcher to obtain at a reasonable cost a photostat copy of the application. The pension records are in the National Archives in Washington, D. C. If you can't personally visit the Archives, it is necessary for you to employ a researcher to search the records for the needed information. Lists of researchers available for assignments in the National Archives and Library of Congress may be had on application to them at Washington, D. C. The Historical Societies in the respective states often times have valuable information about these service men also.

## WAR RECORDS HELP

Most libraries throughout the United States have on their shelves copies of the state histories containing the information about the soldiers of the various wars of the United States, and the earlier Colonial America. If your ancestors date to the earliest days of America they may have been participants in some of the following wars fought here: King William's War, 1690 to 1697, fought mainly in Canada; Queen Anne's War, 1702 to 1713, also fought in Canada; King George's War, 1744 to 1748, conducted on this side of the Atlantic mainly on the island of Cape Breton, between Nova Scotia and Newfoundland, where the French military post of Louisburg was captured by the British in 1745, but returned to the French in 1748; French and Indian War, 1745 to 1763, involving Ohio and Quebec, through which England gained control of everything east of the Mississippi River; The Revolutionary War, 1775 to 1783, which brought about the founding of the United States of America; the War of 1812, declared by the United States against Great Britain, and fought in diverse places, north and south, and brought about no new borders; the Mexican War, 1846 to 1848, which gained us the territory now including several of our western states; the Civil War, 1861 to 1865, the conflict over slavery between the north and the south; the Spanish American War, April 1898 to August 1898, which added to our ownership the Phillippines, Puerto Rico and Cuba.

## CENSUS RECORDS

A census, a registration of the names of all inhabitants, has been taken in most counries since the days of the Roman Empire. It was to comply with the practise that Mary and Joseph left their home in Nazareth to go to Bethlehem to be counted among the decendants fo David, at the time of the birth of Christ. Since then it has been practised in all counties under various names. In Europe it is done under the auspices of the dominant church, as well as by the respective governments.

Since 1790 the government of the United States has conducted a census every ten years. At first only requiring the name of the head of the family, while indicating the number of persons in the family within specific age groups, it now lists not only the complete name but age of each person, his address and vocation or profession, and other information. The 1790 census was taken in all of the seventeen states then existing. Since then each state as it has been created has been included in the succeeding enumerations.

It must be remembered that no census ever taken is absolutely correct, either from the stand point of the information recorded or the completeness of listing all persons living at that time. Enumerators made many mistakes in writing the data required, and many people lived beyong the areas assigned to be counted or were accidently missed. All census records should be used mainly as a guide for clues and not as absolute proof of any point.

The personal information in the 1900 and later censuses is confidential and may be furnished only upon the written request of the person to whom it relates or if deceased, by application signed by a blood relative in the immediate family, surviving spouse, or a beneficiary with legal evidence of such beneficiary relationship. These records for 1900 and later may be obtained by writing for an Age Search Application Form from Personal Service Branch, Bureau of the Census, Pittsburg, Kansas 66762.

NATURALIZATION RECORDS. All foreign born residents of the United States have had the opportunity to become citizens of his nation by observing certain stipulations, which have changed from time to time. A record of these naturalizations have been kept since 1740. If the naturalization took place before 27 September 1906, the search for it should be conducted in the office of the respective county clerk; after that date information may be obtained from the Commissioner of Immigration and Naturalization, Washington 25, D. C.

The naturalization paper contains the following description of the holder: age, height, color, complexion, color of eyes, color of hair, and visible distinguishing marks; name, name of spouse and residence; names, ages and places of residence of minor children; and the name of the country from which the holder came. Earlier naturalization certificates also gave the place and date of entry of holder to the United States. In this way naturalization records direct attention to passenger lists maintained in the National Archives.

## PASSENGER LISTS

Among important books of the earliest arrivals of persons in America are John Camden Hotten's "The Original Lists of persons of Quality; Emigrants, Religious Exiles, Political Rebels, Serving Men Sold for a Term of Years; Apprentices; Children Stolen; Maidens Pressed; and Others Who Went from Great Britain to the American

Plantations 1600-1700, with their Ages, the Localities Where They Formerly Lived in the Mother Country, the Names of the Ships in Which They Embarked, and Other Interesting Particulars,'' printed originally by Mr. Hotten in London, 1847; reprinted: Empire State Book Co., New York.

Charles Edward Banks, ''The Planters of the Commonwealth - a study of the Emigrants and Emigration in Colonial Times: to which are added Lists of Passengers to Boston and the Bay Colony; the Ships which brought them; their English Homes, and the Places of their Settlement in Massachusetts 1620-1640.'' Printed in Boston by the Riverside Press for Houghton Mifflin Co. in Park Street near the Commons, 1930.

Strassburger and Hinke, ''German Pioneers - Original Lists of Arrivals in Philadelphia, 1727 to 1808.'' Three volumes, 1934.

Emigrants via Holland, "Genealogist Magazine (new series).'' Published in London, volumes 23 to 26, 1907 to 1910.

I. Daniel Rupp, ''30,000 Emigrants to Pennsylvania - German, Swiss, Dutch, and French, 1727 to 1776,'' 1931.

Charles Henry Pope, ''Pioneers of Massachusetts,'' 1900.

Walter Allen Knittle, "Early 18th Century Palatine Immigration," 1937.

John C. Evjen, "Scandinavian Immigrants in New York, 1630 to 1674, with Appendices on Settlements in Mexico and South America, 1530 to 1640, and in Canada, 1619 to 1620." 1916.

Jonathan Pearson, "First Settlers of Schenectady, N.Y., 1662 to 1800," 1873.

New York Historical Collection, volume 18, "Roll of Freemen of New York, 1675 to 1866 with indentures of apprenticeships, 1694 to 1707 to 1727."

"Early Settlers of Georgia, prior to 1741," 1949.

"Huguenot Emigration to Virginia," edited by R. A. Brock, Virginia Historical Society Publication, volume five, 1886.

Ora Eugene Monnette, "First Settlers of Piscataway and Woodbridge, N.J., 1664 to 1714, includes source records and genealogical foundations on New England, New Hampshire, Massachusetts; also England and Scotland progenitors with West Indian migrations, especially French Protestants from France before 1700."

Ethel Stenwood Bolton, "Immigrants to New England, 1700 to 1775."

John Farmer, "First Settlers of New England, Genealogical Register of."

Swem, "Virginia Historical Index," (look under emigrants, passengers, etc.) two volumes.

Henry F. Waters, "Genealogical Gleanings in England," two volumes.

Noyes, Libby, Davis, "Genealogical Dictionary of Maine and New Hampshire," five parts.

Indexes to New England Historical and Genealogical Registers.

Donald Lines Jacobus, "Index to Genealogical Periodicals." (In indexes see particular family names or localities of interest to your families.)

Charles Edward Banks, "English Emigrants to New England, 1620 to 1650."

Samuel G. Drake, "Founders of New England as found in the British Archives."

The National Archives also have the passenger lists of vessels from foreign ports arriving in Baltimore, 1820 to 1919; Boston from 1883 to 1899; New Orleans from 1820 to 1897; and New York City from 1820 to 1919; lists of sailors on vessels of American Merchant Marine from 1916 to 1941, and lists of numerous persons formerly employed by various agencies of the American government.

## LAND RECORDS

Of equal value to statistical information, such as birth, marriage and death records, for genealogical recordings are the land records and wills. They reveal, often times, relationships not otherwise recorded. These records are not difficult to obtain. You may have a photostat copy at a reasonable cost from the clerk of the county in which your ancestors lived. To help find the information you must give the time in which they lived there and their full names.

To get similar information from Europe it is best to hire a professional genealogist in the particular country, or find some place where the microfilms of the records are available.

## THE HANDY BOOK FOR GENEALOGISTS

As you start to do research in specific localities you want to know considerable about that part of the country. It will be advantageous for you, for instance, to know about migrations to and from that section - you will want to know about the formation of the counties, where their records are kept, who to write to, etc.

Much of this information is found in the Handy Book for Genealogists, published by The Everton Publishers and probably available through the merchants you purchased this book from. It contains maps of the 50 states and many foreign countries which show the boundries of counties. It tells when the counties were formed and the parent county or territory it was formed from. It lists the county seats and capitals where records of births, marriages and deaths are kept, also who to write to for certified copies or information recorded there. It tells when many of the countries and counties started their records and the type of records available.

This type of information will give you inestimable help in putting you on the right track to get the data you need. You will be able to quickly decide where to go or who to write to to get enlightenment on official records such as wills, deeds, court records, vital statistics, etc. Much other general information on the various states and European countries is given such as population, migrations, libraries, genealogical societies, etc., making it one of the most popular genealogical books ever printed. Almost 45,000 are now in use.

J. S. a professional genealogists of Washington D. C. wrote, ''Send another copy of the Handy Book for Genealogists. Mine is almost worn out from constant use.''

The introduction to THE HANDY BOOK FOR GENEALOGISTS, Fifth Edition has so many good pointers for genealogists, it is being reprinted here almost verbatim. Of course, you will have to consult the book itself to get the information you need but you will find most libraries have a copy. If you do a lot of research you will undoubtedly want a copy of your own. The problems presented and their solutions are typical of thousands of such enigmas you may find as you search for forebears. You should garner many ideas on how to overcome your research perplexities just from the introduction.

INTRODUCTION TO
THE HANDY BOOK FOR GENEALOGISTS
FIFTH EDITION

''As you start to gather information for

your family tree you will undoubtedly find that your American ancestors migrated from place to place. It is a rare thing to find even two or three generations of a family at one location. If they were not in one of the mass movements from Europe to America or from the eastern seaboard on west, they were nevertheless looking for greener pastures and changed their abodes - sometimes so often it is extremely difficult to follow their trails.

"As they moved from one country, state or county to another they usually left records. You must find those records to verify births, deaths, marriages and many other facts regarding their lives and loves. You must follow their trails sometimes backwards and forward. It is not unusual for genealogists to work on both ends of the trail, finally closing the gap, making a complete record of their movements and many other interesting facts about their lives.

"When you start your search for their records you may find some in one state and some in another. It is also possible you will find some of your progenitors living in one place for many years, yet their records are scattered in several counties. This may have been caused by their original counties being divided and subdivided again and again. How to search for these records at one time presented a great challenge, but "The Handy Book for Genealogists" gives answers to thousands of these questions quickly, easily.

"Many of the older genealogists have said they wished they had had this aid when they started research. They had to dig the facts regarding the dates of organization of counties and their parent counties from history books, county commission and legislature minutes books and many other kinds of archival material. By trial and error they found where records were kept, what they revealed, etc. These facts must be known in practically all cases before you can get the information needed to establish your connections.

"Knowing what records are available and who to contact for extracts or copies also presents a tremendous problem as each country, state and county may have different record keeping systems. The county clerk may have the records you need in one county, the city clerk in another, the clerk of the court in another, and the state health department in another. With this book you can quickly decide where to write for what records.

"To assist you in the use of the information you have in this volume let us illustrate with some hypothetical cases:

## 1. STATE HISTORIES

"Tradition holds that one of your great grand parents was born in Missouri in 1811. You check the history of Missouri in "The Handy Book" and find it did not become a territory until 1812 - that from 1805 to 1812 it was part of Louisiana Territory. Therefore it would be unlikely that Missouri would have a record about him or his parents in 1811. If you wanted to start a search, the place to look would be in the Louisiana records. Of course, you might find he was not born in Missouri or in 1811 - that his parents brought him from another state as a babe or any one of a dozen other possibilities. One sure thing, you would know that the Territory of Missouri was not created until 1812, one year after his traditional birth, and prior to that time that section belonged to the Territory of Louisiana.

## 2. COUNTY HISTORIES

"Suppose you had a progenitor who was one of the first settlers at Key West, Florida. He took his family there in 1822 but died in 1823 leaving his wife and children. You want to know if there is a will, record of real estate, or any other contemporary record about him in the county records. You find that Key West is the county seat of Monroe County, but none of their records help you.

You wonder if something might be found in adjoining counties but your search is fruitless in six or eight neighboring counties. Finally you learn about the "Handy Book for Genealogists," You turn to page 40 and find that Monroe County was formed in 1824 from St. John County, one year after the death of your forefather. A further check reveals that St. Augustine is the county seat of St. John County and it is almost on the other side of the state, over 375 miles from Key West. You go to the records at St. Augustine and there find just what you want.

"Next you search for the records of a forebear who lived and died in Ford County, Illinois. He was 75 years old at his death in 1869 - making his birth date ca. 1794. You have reason to believe he was born at or near his place of death and would like to know everything possible about him from the county records. You check Ford County on page 59 of "The Handy Book" and find it was formed in 1859 from Clark County. Going back you find that Clark was formed in 1859 from Crawford which was formed from Edwards in 1815. In turn Edwards was formed in 1814 from Madison and Gallatin, they being formed in 1812. St. Clair, which was formed from the N.W. Territory in 1790, was the parent county of Madison. Randolph, formed from St. Clair and the

N.W. Territory in 1795, was the parent county of Gallatin.

"You must search the records of six or seven counties to be sure you have all that can be found about a man who supposedly lived all his life within the confines of one county: Ford 1869-1814; Clark 1850-1819; Crawford 1819-1815; Edwards 1815-1814. Then Madison 1814-1812; St. Clair 1812-1795 or Gallatin 1814-1812; Randolph 1812-1795. It might pay to do further investigating to establish whether your research should go to Madison or Gallatin Counties. It undoubtedly would not be both.

### 3. LIBRARIES

"One of your ancestors came from Connecticut. What library might have records on his life? You check the list of libraries on page 28 and find quite a number you can write to for information. You also find several books listed which could be extremely helpful in your progenitor search.

### 4. MAPS

"You are searching the records for an early pioneer of Colorado County, Texas. You note this county was created in 1836 but on writing to the County Clerk, he informs you that the county was not finally organized until 40 years later, 1876, and practically none of their records go beyond the organization date. You look at the map of Texas and find that Austin, Fayette, Fort Bend, Jackson, Lavaca and Wharton Counties surround Colorado County and a further check shows they were all created about the same time or shortly after Colorado. It might be well to check with neighboring county clerks to ascertain if they have some record of your ancestor. Occasionally persons would travel to an adjoining county for a marriage or other important business if it could not be taken care of in their own county.

"A new feature of this edition is that the maps of all the states show the adjoining counties in neighboring states. Thus you can follow migrations with much greater ease than heretofore.

"You follow the trail of one of your ancestors in his westward trek through Virginia. It starts at James City with a year or two or three stop in each of the following counties: Henrico, Buckingham, Roanoke and Scott. Here you lose the trail. You have reason to believe he moved across the line to Tennessee. You locate Scott County on the map and you find bordering it on the south the Tennessee counties of Hancock, Hawkins and Sullivan - the three counties you will have to search to pick up the trail again.

## 5. COUNTY RECORDS

"A questionnaire was sent to every county

clerk or clerk of court in the U.S. asking for information about the records in their custody. About half of them returned the questionnaire. Many gave information which should be helpful in searching county records. This information is included in this edition with the other county data. For instance you turn to Arkansas on page 11 and find that Arkansas County is the first county listed. Under this county you find: (Co Clk has pro rec from 1809; Cir Clk has div & civ ct rec from 1803, war ser discharge from 1917.) Interpreted this says: County Clerk has probate records from 1809; Circuit Clerk has divorce and civil court records from 1803 and war service discharges from 1917.

### 6. GENEALOGISTS' CHECK LIST OF HISTORICAL RECORDS SURVEY.

''Surveys of public record archives were conducted in most states during 1936 to 1943 by the Works Progress Administration (WPA), a government agency. For example, inventories were made of the federal archives in all the states, of state, some county and municipal archives, transcripts of some public archives, directories of church archives and religious publications, guides to public vital statistics records and depositories of manuscript collections, check lists of American imprints, and various other surveys and listings of records and archives of interest to different types of researchers.

"A great many of these records, as you will note, are vital to genealogical research. But very few of the WPA publications give full transcripts - they only name the records available in the respective archives. Quite often they tell the condition of the records, where they were stored when the survey was made, and dates of commencement and conclusion of the records. The records themselves must be examined to gain the information.

"However, you may save a lot of time in your data search by first consulting the check list, and then the survey, inventory or transcript to find out the existence of buried or piled up records in some county courthouse basement or attic, which may give contemporary evidence regarding the life of your ancestor.

"Of course, only a small portion of all available records and archives were surveyed, but that which was completed is a great help in locating records for research-finding what may be available - what the records contain, etc.

"Many times one will find unusual and extremely valuable records for genealogical research in county or other archives which are not common. A search should be made in each place to see if such records as naturalization papers, apprenticeship records, special tax assessments, and many other out-of-the-ordinary records are available, as well as the usual wills, deeds, court and vital records.

"From the Genealogists Check List of the Historical Records Survey you can quickly determine if a survey was made by the WPA. Then you should consult the survey to ascertain what records are available in that archive - the usual and the unusual. You will then know what to look for if you can visit the place personally or what to write for if you can't.

"A check list of these publications was published by the WPA according to the type of publication. Sometimes it takes a lot of searching to find all the records which might be listed of one state or locality. Many of the publications are of little or no value to genealogists since they pertain to such things as reports and records of the Treasury department and other federal agencies none of which have any personal records. They are of no value to the genealogist.

"At the suggestion of Meredith B. Colket, Jr., for many years director of the Institute for Genealogical Research, sponsored by the American University and the National Ar-

chives, George B. Everton, Sr., of the
Everton Publishers undertook the assign-
ment of making a rearranged check list of
these WPA publications. Almost 2000 books
were examined and evaluated as to their
genealogical value. The ones of no value to
genealogists were eliminated from the list.
Then the list was rearranged according to
states, putting all publications of a state
together. Thus, if you are searching for records of Missouri you can now find them all
grouped together,    making it possible to
quickly determine if the records of any particular county, city, church or federal agency
in Missouri was surveyed for records of a
genealogical nature. If so, then you should
try to get the publication to determine if any
records might be available which would
assist you.

"Of course, as with most records, you will
find some of the listed publications of greater
value than others. For instance, Ship Registers and Enrollments have only a slight value
to genealogists. Nevertheless, the names of
the owners and captains of these ships are
easy to check in the good indices and at
times this may prove to be the only record
you can find of these people. You may also
find clues as to where other records may be
found. So don't be discouraged if some of the
publications don't produce the information

you need. Persistence is a virtue no genealogist can afford to overlook.

"Every state or region had a designated depository of unpublished material which also may have many of the publications. An exchange was made at the time of printing whereby copies were supposed to be sent to each region or state depository. The depositories of unpublished materials - that which was in preparation for publication at the time the project was abandoned - are listed in the rearranged check list. Many libraries also have fair collections of the WPA Historical Records Survey Publications. At one time the Library of Congress acted as an exchange station, distributing surplus copies to other libraries and depositories. The staff of the National Archives Library, Washington 25, D. C., under the direction of Miss Grace Quimby have also endeavored to gather a complete set, but still lack some numbers. They also have a few surplus copies they would be happy to exchange with other libraries or depositories, especially if they could fill in the ones they lack.

"So you may find a copy of the publication you need close by, or you may have to do some searching. Check with your local library first and extend your search from there. If you can locate the publications pertinent to the area and time of your ancestor you may save many hours of tedious labor, as they will quickly show you what records are available in each archive where surveys were made."

## EARLY SPELLING OF NAMES

Every surname may be spelled in several ways. The researcher should try to know all of them. You may be proud of your family name - justly so - but do not imagine that it has always been spelled as it is now.

As a warning to tyro researchers to weigh carefully the spelling of early family names, let us recall that the familiar Kress name has been written in twenty-one different ways by priests and recorders of Europe namely, Krehs, Kresz, Kresze, Kreshe, Kresse, Kresso, Crezzo, Creso, Cresso, Chresos, Chrehse, Cresse, Chreshe, Crese, Cresze, Cres, Cras, Cresen, Creseno and Cresonis.

What is the reason for so many different spellings of names? Not so many hundreds of years ago few people could read and fewer could write. The spelling of a family name was not of any particular interest to members of the family. The minister or the lawyer or the landlord or the county clerk spelled the names that came to them in their line of duty as they sounded to them. Any way they were spelled drew no comment from the family members.    It is not particularly strange that each one who wrote the name may have spelled it in a new way, a different way. The same name may be spelled one way in the church record, another way in a deed, a third way in a will and a fourth way in the cemetery record, etc. etc.

Whatever names you are interested in try to find out the many different ways they may be spelled. When you come across the different varieties in your research, don't toss any of them aside, but take note of them and keep them in your record. They may come in handy some time. If you pass up any of the different varieties of spelling, you may have to retrace your steps later and pick them up. (See pages 5, 67-70).

## WHENCE CAME SURNAMES

Strange as it may seem, surnames have not always been used to designate a particular family. Early Bible characters, for instance, had only one name, such as Seth, Noah, Abraham. It was not until the days of Moses, when the population had grown into millions, that it became necessary to distinguish individuals having the same given name. There was Korah, the son of Izhar, the son of Kohath, the son of Levi, recognizing four generations; there was Joshua the son of Nun; Jair the son of Manasseh. By the time of Christ, the custom of adding surnames had become common. We read of Simon BarJona.  The word Bar meaning son, it would be Simon son of Jona, or, to put the later Scandinavian touch to it, Simon Jonasson.  About that time are also noted the locality and the character descriptive names, such as Simon of Cyrene, and Simon the Zealot.

In the Roman heyday we find the artistocratic families rather generous with their use of names, giving each person a Christian name, a clan name and a family name. Thus we meet Caius Julius Caesar, Marcus Tullius Cicero, Publius Vergilius Maro, and many other similar three-part names.

With the fall of the Roman culture and the ascendency of barbarianism names went back to the simple standard.

According to Prof. Osborne J. P. Widtsoe, on whose "An Introduction to the study of English Surnames" these paragraphs are based, surnames have originated in the following ways; patronymic, derived from the father's name; local, from the designation of the property owned, or from some local peculiarity of the home; occupational, from trades or occupations followed; official, from some rank or office held; or nicknames.

France adopted surnames about 1000 A.D.; England, at least among the leading families, about the time of William the Conquerer. The Doomesday Book reveals the early use of surnames. Before that time it was common to speak of a man as the son of his father. In Wales was used the word ap, meaning son of, as ap Rice, ap Evan, etc. When ap came before a vowel sound, the two words were combined, resulting in a new name, as Pugh from Ap-Hugh, Price from Ap-Rice, Bowen from Ap-Owen, Pritchard from Ap-Richard, Powell from Ap-Howell, etc.

Similarly surnames were derived from the French prefix fitz, coming from the Latin filius meaning son, such as Fitzsimon, Fitzgerald, Fitzpatrick, etc., or from the Gallic mac, also meaning son, resulting in McFarland, Mac Donald, McMaster, etc.

The Norman-French diminutives ot and et have formed many surnames, such as

Emmett from little Emma, Eliot from little Elias, Marriot from little Mary, Wilmot from little William; also the diminutives on and en have formed Alison from the son of little Alice; Huggins, the son of little Hugh, Robinson, the son of little Robert.

More names have been derived from localities than anything else. John of Gaunt (Chent) became John a Gaunt, and then John Gaunt; or Henry of Hull became Henry a Hull and then Henry Hull; Jack of London became Jack a London and finally Jack London; Richard of Lancaster, Richard a Lancaster, Richard Lancaster.

Contraction of words have created these cycles in names: John at the Brook, John atte Brook, John at Brook, John a Brook, John Brook. When studying the old original records, it is well to remember that the name will no doubt appear in one or the other of these designations. One who lived near some oak trees first became atte Oaks, n Oaks, Noakes or Nokes. It is easy to see the derivation of Bywater, Bywood, By-the-way, Bygates, Byatts, or Fieldman, Fielding, Bridgeman, Beecher, Beechman, Churcher, Churchman, Kirkman, Wood, At-wood, Openshaw (an open small woody covert), Ogden, (hog den), Swinden, Graves,

Cluff, Knowles (tree-less gently-rising grassy slopes). Tillers of the soil have been named Farmer, Plowman, Gardiner, Tillman, Mower, Cropper, Dyker, Dykeman, Drayner, Marler, Akerman, Beeman, Beaman, Woodman, Hewer, Herd, Hurd, Heard, Stotherd, Stoddard, Shepherd, Goddard, (goat herd) Swinart, Hoggart, Soward, Thatcher, Hillyer (from hillier, a roofer), Tyler, Slater, Slatter, Cotter, Cotterel, Cotterell, Miller, Milne, Milner, Mills, Smith, Wright, Cartwright, Wagoner, Driver, Chapman, Chipman (the buyer), Packman, Paxman, Weaver, Wolman, Woolsey, Webster, (female weaver), Dyer, Brewer, Brewster, Tapper, Tapster, Potter, Crocker, Chandler (candlemaker), Forester, Forster, Foster, Woodruff, (guard of the woods), etc.

## CLUES IN NAMES

Unusual Christian names often furnish a clue to which family a group may belong. For instance, one of the early Hales was named Jonathan. This Jonathan has thousands of descendants now, scattered far and wide. Wherever you find descendants of this Jonathan you are apt to find a Jonathan Hale in the proximity. In unrelated Hales families this is more than likely not the case. There are some names, such as John, Thomas, James, etc., that are common in almost all families and one could not get a reliable clue from such. Of course, care must be exercised even with the most unusual names as there is no proof unless corroborative evidence is found.

When you find a record of a name that sounds like a surname, that is often the surname of his mother or his grandmother. This clue is worth investigating.

## APPROXIMATING DATES

Quite often you may find among your relatives one whose birth date is not available. To place such a one in relation to other names on your chart it is advisable to use an approximate date of birth. It is always well to take into consideration the marriage date of the parents, if that is available, and the birth dates of other children in the family.

Statistics have been gathered from thousands of families in various countries and the following figures represent the average of the whole group. The average age of fathers at the birth of the first child is 26 years and of mothers it is 22 years. If you have the birth date of only one child and do not know which child it is, first or a later one, the average age of the father will be 32 years and of the mother 28 years. Remember that these figures are averages only and will be wrong more often than right. Count the approximate age at marriage at 25 years for the man and 21 years for the woman. If you have the death date you are fortunate but you cannot approximate the birth date from that unless the age at death is given. Approximate dates should be marked ''about'' and it is well to indicate how the approximation was arrived at.

## NOTES

RELATIONSHIP CHART

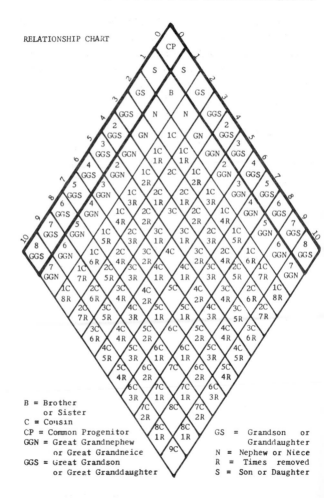

B = Brother
    or Sister
C = Cousin
CP = Common Progenitor
GGN = Great Grandnephew
    or Great Grandneice
GGS = Great Grandson
    or Great Granddaughter

GS = Grandson    or
    Granddaughter
N = Nephew or Niece
R = Times removed
S = Son or Daughter

# III

# Relationships

If you have difficulties in figuring relationships on your lineal or collateral lines, close or distant, you will find the chart on the opposite page a quick solution to all these troubles. This chart, prepared especially for this publication, shows the relationship of descendants to a progenitor, also the relationship between the progenitor's descendants in any combination of degrees from him down to and including the tenth generation. Though there have been other systems of figuring relationships this is the most universal, being used in all courts of law and by major genealogical societies.

## HOW TO USE RELATIONSHIP CHART

You will note that the two upper columns are outlined in heavy lines. These are the common progenitor and his descendants. "CP" stands for common progenitor, the one who is the head of the two lines of descendants. "S" is his son or daughter as the case may be; "GS" his grandson or granddaughter; "GGS" his great grandson or great granddaughter; "2GGS" his second

great grandson or second great granddaughter, and so on down to his eighth great
grandson or granddaughter.

All the diamonds inside these heavy lines
show the relationship between his descendants.    By following columns ''1'' from
both sides of the chart we find they cross
on the ''B'' diamond, showing that the sons
of the common progenitor are brothers.
By following columns ''2'' to the center we
find they cross at the ''1C'' diamond, in
dicating that grandsons of the common progenitor are first cousins to each other.
And so on down: his great grandsons are
second cousins; his second great grandsons are third cousins; his third great
grandsons are fourth cousins, etc.

To this point few people have trouble
in figuring relationships.    It is when they
start to figure the ''cousinship'' and ''times
removed'' that they have difficulty. But with
this chart you will find no trouble with any
combination up to the tenth generation, and
by following the pattern set by this chart
you can go as many generations as you desire.    Say you want to figure your relationship to a distant cousin.    You are eight
generations removed from the common
progenitor, or his sixth great grandson.

Your "distant cousin" is six generations removed or his fourth great grandson on another line. To figure your exact relationship simply follow columns "8" on the one side and "6" on the other to where they cross and you find "5C 2R" indicating you are fifth cousins twice removed.

If you want to find your relationship to the son of your fifth great grandfather, follow columns "1" and "7" which show you are his fourth great grandnephew (4 GGN). Likewise, you are a first cousin six times removed (1C 6R) to the grandson of your sixth great grandfather.

As additional aids to understanding terms used in relationship descriptions we give the following:

The parents of your father or mother are your grandfather or grandmother and you are a grandson to them. (GS)

The parents of your grandfather or grandmother are your great grandparents and you are a great grandson to them. (GGS)

The parents of your great grandmother or great grandfather are your second great grandparents and you are a second great grandson to them, etc., etc., (2GGS)

The children of your brothers and sisters

are your nephews and nieces (N) and you are uncle or aunt to them.

The children of your nieces and nephews are your grand nieces or grandnephews (GN) and you are granduncle to them.

The children of your grandnephews and grandnieces are your great grandnephews or great grandnieces (GGN) and you are great granduncle to them.

Your father's brother or sister is your uncle or aunt and you are a nephew or niece to them. (N)

The children of your uncle or aunt are your first cousins and you are also their first cousin. (1C)

The children of your first cousins are are first cousins once removed to you and you are the same to them. (1C 1R)

The son of your third great grandfather is your second great granduncle and you are a second great grandnephew or niece to him.

The children of your second cousins are your second cousins once removed and you are the same to them.

The grandchildren of your second cousins are your second cousins twice removed and you are the same to them.

The great grand children of your second cousins are your second cousins thrice removed and you are the same to them.

The second great grandchildren of your second cousins are your second cousins four times removed and you are the same to them.

A simple formula for figuring cousin relationships by the above method is this: Call the common ancestor ''O'' and count down to the subjects, subtract one from the smaller of the two figures - this is the cousin relationship. Then subtract the smaller number from the larger and this gives you the times removed. Example: one subject is seven steps down from the common ancestor, the other is four steps down - one from four is three, so the cousinship is third cousins, and four from seven is three (three times removed) making them third cousins three times removed (3c3r).

Another example:
Subject No. 1 is 9 steps down from the common ancestor.
Subject No. 2 is 6 steps down from the common ancestor.
6 - 1 = 5th cousin. 9 - 6 = 3 times removed.
So they are fifth cousins three times removed. (5c3r).

Of course, if the steps down from the common ancestor are the same you simply subtract 1 from the number and it gives you their cousinship and there are no times removed to be figured. Remember also that the common ancestor is never counted when figuring the steps down to the subject, just as it appears on the chart on page 128.

## NOTES

# IV
# Dictionary Of Genealogical Words, Terms And Abbreviations

This dictionary of genealogical terms and abbreviations is the largest ever presented to aid the novice or professional genealogist. It includes Latin, law, general words and phrases, abbreviations and hundreds of words from the languages of most of the European countries, all arranged in alphabetical order for ease of use. The inclusion of the many foreign words with the English is a new innovation for this type of publication but we are sure it will be much easier for you to find their meanings with this arrangement, especially when you find them interspersed with English as is sometimes the case.

References are made in the case of some terms as to where additional information may be found. A system has been devised to indicate which abbreviations are recognized by Webster's New International Dictionary and those not officially approved at this time on many of the words. If you find an asterisk (*) preceeding a word you will know that word is not approved officially at this time. Where you do not find the asterisk, the word may or may not be approved. Many abbreviations not approved officially are in general use today by genealogists and may some day receive recognition through constant use. Others are abbreviations of the past - which at times give the researcher considerable trouble because of their obscure meanings. Latin terms and abbreviations are included because it was the dominant language of schools, courts and churches during olden times and its influence is still felt in many records of modern times.

In the case of some words, only those meanings pertaining to genealogy are listed. No attempt has been made to segregate the meanings as to whether the word used in that sense would be a noun, verb, verb transitive or intransitive, adjective, adverb, etc. In some cases only the old or obscure meanings are given.

The following dictionaries were used in the compilation: "Webster's New International Dictionary", Second Edition, Unabridged, G. C. Merriam Co., 1949; "The American College Dictionary", Random

House, 1951; "Handy Dictionary of the Latin and English Languages", David McKay Co., Philadelphia, 1948; "Cassell's Latin Dictionary", Funk and Wagnalls Co., N. Y. 1953 printing. The books listed under "Explanation of Terms and Symbols" were also used as well as others, including "Proving Your Pedigree" by Archibald F. Bennett, published by the Deseret Sunday School Union Board, 1955 and "A Basic Course in Genealogy" Vol. 1, by Gardner, Harland and Smith, published 1958, Bookcraft, Inc.

Your comments, suggestions and corrections will be welcomed for future editions.

## EXPLANATION OF TERMS AND SYMBOLS

\* - the asterisk indicates abbreviations not recognized in Webster's New International Dictionary, Second Edition, G. C. Merriam Co., 1949. Examples: 1. adm.; \*admin.; admr.; admstr., indicates all except "admin." are recognized as proper abbreviations of "administrator". 2. in the case of the abbreviation "an.", you will find listed \*annus; anno. This indicates that "an." is recognized for anno but not for annus. 3. k. \*killed; king., indicates that "k." is a proper abbreviation for king

and not killed. Nevertheless, you will find
in some of the old records that ''k'' is
used for killed. It may be used for other
words as well, as it would be almost
impossible to gather all abbreviations that
have ever been used in genealogical records - attempt has been made only to
gather and list the more common ones.
In the abbreviations of countries, states,
cities, etc., no attempt has been made to
distinguish those recognized and not recognized.

ABC - ''The ABC's of American Genealogical Research'', by E. Kay Kirkham, published by Deseret Book Co., 1955.

(Aus) - Austria.
(Be) - Belgium.
(Can) - Canada.
(D) - Danish or Denmark.
(Du) - Dutch or Netherlands.
(E) - English or England.
(Fi) - Finnish or Finland.
(Fr) - French or France.
(G) - German or Germany.
GGR - ''A Guide for Genealogical Re-
search'', by Archibald F. Bennett, pub-
lished by Genealogical Society of the
Church of Jesus Christ of Latter-day
Saints, 1951.

1953 HB – "The 1953 Handy Book for Genealogists", by George B. Everton and Gunnar Rasmuson, published by the Everton Publishers, 1953.

(Ic) – Icelandic or Iceland.

(Ire) – Irish or Ireland.

(It) – Italian or Italy.

(L) – a Latin word or phrase.

(Ne) – Netherlands.

(No) – Norwegian or Norway.

p. – page.     pp. – pages.

(q.v.) – the Latin abbreviation for "quode vide", meaning "which see".

(qq.v.) – the Latin plural of "which see". In other words when you find (q.v.) following a word, if you will turn to that word you will find additional information on the subject; (qq.v.) means to look up the words preceeding.

(Sc) – Scotch or Scotland.

(Sp) – Spanish or Spain.

SR – "Search and Research", by Noel C. Stevenson, copyright 1951 by Forrest Cool.

(Sw) – Swedish or Sweden.

SYA – "Searching for Your Ancestors," by Gilbert Harry Doane, published by University of Minnesota, second printing, 1952.

(Sz) – Swiss or Switzerland.

(W) – Welch or Wales.

**WMIA** - "Ways and Means of Identifying Ancestors", by Evan L. Reed, published by Ancestral Publishing & Supply Co., 1947.

NOTES

## A

a. - *administration; annus (qq.v.); about; age.

a. - acre, acres

A./Agder. (No) - Aust/Agder

aar (D) (No) - year

ab. - *abbey (q.v.); about

ab. (W) - son

A.-Bard. (Ic) - Auster-Bardastrandarsysla

abavus (L) - second great grandfather; ancestor.

abbey - a monastery ruled by an abbot or a convent ruled by an abbess. Abbr. - *ab., abb.

abbr.; abbrev. - abbreviated; abbreviation.

abjure - to renounce upon oath; to forswear; disavow. To abjure the realm was to swear, or take oath, to leave the country and never to return without leave of the king.

abjurer - one who abjures (q.v.).

abortivus (L) - stillborn.

Abp. - Archbishop

abruptio (L) - breaking off; divorce.

abstract - a summary of the important points of a book or manuscript.

Abstract Books - books which list individual entries chronologically by district land office. (ABC p. 76).

abstract of title - a summary of the history of the title to land, showing liabilities and charges subject to the same.

abstract of will - a summary or an epitome of the will. In the genealogical sense an abstract of a will gives only the parts of the will which help in determining relationships, locations, etc.

abt. - *about

Abu; Abou - literally, father; the first element in many Arabic proper names. Sometimes abbreviated to Bu.

abuela (Sp) - grandmother

abuelo (Sp) - grandfather

A.C. Ante Christum (L) - before Christ.

Acadia - the original name of Nova Scotia.

acc. - according (to); account; accompanied.

ach (W) - pedigree

achievement - (Her.) an escutcheon with its helm, crest, mantle, supporters and motto.

achter-kleindochter (Du) - great-granddaughter

achter-kleinzoon (Du) - great-grandson

ackd. - *acknowledged

ad. - addatur (q.v.)

AD. - *archdeaconry (q.v.).

A.D. - Anno Domini (q.v.).

a.d. - ante diem (q.v.).

adcon. - *archdeacon; *archdeaconry (qq.v.).

add. - addatur; adde (qq.v.).

addatur (L) - let there be added; add. Abbr. - ad.; add.

adde (L) - add. Abbr. - add.

adj. - *adjoining; adjourned

adlig (G) - noble

ad loc. - ad locum (q.v.).

ad locum (L) - to or at the place. Abbr. - ad loc.

adm.; admin. - administrator (q.v.); administrative.

administration - the settling of an estate by one appointed by the proper court. Abbr. - *a.; *adm.; *adom.

administrator - the person appointed by court to settle an estate, either of one who is alive and proved incompetent, or an intestate (q.v.). He differs from an executor as he is appointed by the court, whereas the executor is appointed by the deceased and approved by the court. Should an executor be proved incompetent or otherwise unable to serve, the court may appoint an administrator in his place. Abbr. - adm.; *admin.; admr.; adms.; admstr.

admr. - administrator (q.v.).

adom. - *administration (q.v.).

adopt - to take voluntarily a child of other parents to be in the place of, or as one's own child.

adoption - the act of adopting.

ad patres (L) - gathered to his father's; dead.

a.d.s. - autographed document signed.

ae.; aet. - aetatis (q.v.).

Aegidius (L) - Giles

Aelizia (L) - Alice

äeltester, aelteste (G) - oldest, eldest, Elder.

aetas (L) - life-time; age; generation.

aetat. - aetatis (q.v.).

aetatis (L) - of age. Abbr. - ae.; aet.; aetat.

aetatula (L) - very tender childhood.

affidavit - a sworn statement in writing, sworn to before proper authority. Abbr. - afft.

affinity - relationship by marriage between a husband and his wife's blood relations. Or between a wife and her husbands blood relations; in-law relationship.

afft. - affidavit (q.v.)

afsd. - *aforesaid.

aft. - *after; afternoon.

âge (Fr) - age.

agée (Fr) - aged.

agnates - a kinsman whose connection is traceable exclusively through ma-

# GENEALOGICAL DICTIONARY

les; any male relative by the father's side.

A.H. - Anno Hegirae, first year of Moslem era (A. D. 622).

A.H. - Anno Hebraico (q.v.).

ahne (G) - ancestor

ahnentafel (G) - pedigree; a table of ancestors.

A.-Hun. (Ic) - Austur-Hunavatnssysla.

äidinsetä (Fi) - granduncle

äidintäiti (Fi) - grandaunt

ail hendaid (W) - 2nd great grandfather

âiné; âinée (Fr) - eldest

äiti (Fi) - mother

Akerhs. (No) - Akershus

Ala. - Alabama

Alanus (L) - Alan

Alberedus; Aluredus (L) - Alfred

alder (D) (No) - age

âlder (Sw) - age.

äldst, älst (Sw) - eldest

aldste (D) - eldest

Alesia, Aleysia (L) - Alice.

alias - another name; an assumed name.

Alienora (L) - Eleanor

alien - a foreigner

alienus (L) - another's; foreign; contrary; averse; hostile; insane; distracted.

alius (L) - another; other.

alleg. - *allegiance (q.v.).

allegiance - the relation of a feudal vassal, or leige man to his superior, or liege lord (qq.v.); the tie

or obligation of a subject to his sovereign or government. Abbr. - *alleg.

Aloysius (L) - Lewis

Alpes-Marit. (Fr) - Alpes-Maritimes

als. - alias

alt (G) - old

Alta. - Alberta.

alter (G) - age.

alumnus (L) - foster son.

Älvsbg. (Sw) - Älvsborg

Amabilia (L) - Mabel.

amateur genealogist - one who cultivates the science or study of genealogy as an avocation for personal pleasure or gratification, with out thought of monetary reward; not a professional. The matter of skill or ability has no weight, necessarily, in determining amateur or professional standing.

Ambrosius (L) - Ambrose

Amia (L) - Amy

amicus (L) - friend, ally, lover; patron; counsellor

amita (L) - father's sister (aunt).

amita magna (L) - grandfather's sister; grandaunt.

amt (D) - county

amt (No) - older name for county

an. - *annus; anno (qq.v.).

Anabilia (L) - Annabel

anc. - *ancestor.

ancêtres (Fr) - ancestors

ancestor - one from whom a person is descended; any person of lineal or collateral relationship from whom property has been derived by descent. (An "X" is used in front of a name of a child on some family group sheets to designate one's ancestor.)

ancestress - a woman ancestor.

anciano (Sp) - aged

ancient district (Sc) - area larger than a county, as Galloway (included the countries of Wigton, Kirkudbright and southern parishes of Ayrshire), or Angus (included Forfarshire and part of Perthshire).

An. Do. - *Anno Domini (q. v.)

Andreas (L) - Andrew.

Anetavle (D) - pedigree

anghyfreithlon (W) - illegitimate.

Angl. - Anglican, Anglicized.

Angl. (W) - Anglesey.

Anicetis Civitas (L) - In Dorsetshire.

änka (Sw) - widow.

änkeman (Sw) - widower.

änkling (Sw) - widower.

anmhriod (W) -unmarried.

Anna (L) - Anne.

année (Fr) - year.

anni (L) - years.

anno (It) - year.

anno (L) - in the year. Abbr. - an.

Anno Domini (L) - in the (specified) year of the Christian Era. Abbr. - A.D.; An. Do.; *Anno. Dom.

Anno Hebraico (L) - in the (specified) Hebrew year. (Add 3760 to the Christian year). Abbr. - A.H.

Anno Hegirae -first year of Moslem era (A.D. 622) Abbr. - A.H.

annor (L) - see annus.

Anno Regina Regis or Reginae (L) - in the year of the King's or Queen's reign. Abbr. - A.R.R.

anno regni (L) - in the year of the reign. Abbr. -a.r.

annosus (L) - aged, old.

annos vixit (L) - he lived (so many) years. Abbr. - a.v.

annus (L) - year; season; year's produce; age. Abbr. - a.; *an.; *ano.; (also anno, annor).

ano. - *another; *annus (q. v.).

año (Sp) - year.

Ano. Dom. - *Anno Domini (q.v.).

anonyma (L) - stillborn daughter.

anonymus (L) - stillborn son.

antavla (Sw) - pedigree.

ante (L) - before.

antecedent - one's ancestry, past life, education, etc.

ante diem (L) - before the day. Abbr. - a.d.

ante-hac (L) - before this time; earlier.

antenato (It) - ancestor.

antenupital contract - a contract made before marriage, usually made in contemplation of marriage, esp. between the parties as to their property rights.

antepasados (Sp) - ancestors.

Anthonius (L) - Anthony.

Antona Borealis (L) - Northampton.

Antwerp. (Bel) - Antwerpen

anus (L) - old woman.

ap (W) - son of.

Apaunaris Civitas (L) - In Devonshire.

app. - apprentice (q.v.); *approximately.

App. Div. - Appelate Division

Appellate Court - Court of Appeals. Abbr. - App.

apprd - *appeared.

apprd. - *apprised.

apprentice - one who is bound by indentures or by legal agreement to serve another person for a certain time, with the view to learning an art or a trade. Abbr. - app.

apprs. - *apprisers.

apud (L) - at; by; near; with; among; in; before; in the time of.

a quo (L) - of or from whom

år (Sw) - year.

a.r. - anno regni (q.v.).

Araldus (L) - Harold.

Aramis, Aranus Civitas (L) - Dorsetshire.

arbiter - judge, umpire.

archaic script - handwriting, or characters used in handwriting, belonging to or having the characteristics of an earlier or more primitive time.

archdeacon - the chief deacon. Abbr. - Archd; *arches (pl.).

archdeaconry - the office, state, tenure or residence of the archdeacon; a subdivision of a diocese (Church of England). Abbr. - * AD; *adcon.

arches. - *archdeacons (q.v.).

archididascalus (L) - headmaster.

archives - places in which public records or historic documents are kept; public records or documents preserved as evidence of facts.

archivist - a custodian of archives or records.

Arcturus, Artorius (L) - Arthur.

ardal (W) - country.

arg. - argentum (q.v.).

argentum (L) (Her.) - silver.

Ariz. - Arizona

Ark. - Arkansas.

armifer (L) - bearing arms or weapons; shield bearer.

armiger - formerly, an armorbearer, as of a knight; an esquire. Later, one next in degree to a knight, and entitled to armorial bearings.

armiger(i) (L) - an armour bearer. .

armigerous - bearing (heraldic) arms.

arms - the hereditary ensigns armorial of a family, consisting of figures and colors borne in shields, banners, etc., as marks of dignity and distinction. (GGR, pp. 217-223).

Arn. (Ic) - Arnessysla.

A.R.R. - Anno Regina Regis (q.v.).

arrière grand-mère (Fr) - great-grandmother.

arrière grand-père (Fr) - great-grandfather.

2me arrière grand-père (Fr) - 2nd great-grand father.

3me arrière grand-père (Fr) - 3rd great- grand father.

4me arrière grand-père (Fr) - 4th great- grand-father.

arrière petite-fille (Fr) - great-granddaughter.

arrière petit-fils (Fr) - great-grandson.

arrondissement (Fr) - division of a department or county (in Belgium a county; unit for the registration of vital statistics).

arrondissement (Ne) - civil district.

ascendant - an ancestor (opposed to descendant).

A. Skaft. (Ic) - Austur Skaftafellssysla.

A. Sonbg. (D) - Aabenraa Sønderborg.

atavus (L) - great great grandfather's father; third great grandfather; ancestor.

atque (L) - and; and also or even; and too; as much as if; than; yet; nevertheless

atqui (L) - but; yet; notwithstanding; however; rather.

attest - to bear witness to; to certify; to affirm to be true or genuine.

attorney, letter of - see power of attorney.

atturnatus (L) - attorney.

atty. - attorney.

Augusta Trinobantum, Augusta (L) - London.

Augustinus (L) - Austin.

authentic - having a genuine origin or authority, as opposed to one that is

false, fictitious, counter-
fiet, or apocryphal; gen-
uine.

autobiography - a biography
written by the subject of
it; memoirs of one's life
written by oneself.

a.v. - annos vixit (q.v.).

ava, avola (It) - grand-
mother.

avia (L) - grandmother.

aviomies (Fi) - husband.

avioton (Fi) - illegitimate.

avo, avola (It) - grand-
father.

Avona Mediterranea, sive
Borealis (L) - Northamp-
ton.

avunculus (L) - (maternal)
uncle.

avunculus major (L) -
grandmother's brother;
granduncle.

avus (L) - grandfather; ancestor.

az., azure (Her.) - blue.

B

b. - born; *birth; bachelor
(q.v.); brother (q.v.).

ba. - *baptized (q.v.).

baban (W) - infant.

baby (Du) - infant.

bach. - bachelor (q.v.).

bachelor - a knight who followed the standard of an-
other, either because of
his youth or of having too
few vassals of his own;
a man who has not mar-

ried. Abbr. - b.; bach;
*bachr.

bachgen (W) - boy.

bachr. - *bachelor (q.v.).

bad (Ger) - Bath, Spa, health
resort.

baer (Ic) - city.

bambino (It) - infant.

banns - a notice of a pro-
posed marriage, pro-
claimed in a church or
other place prescribed by
law, in order that anyone
may object, if he knows
any impediment to the
marriage. Also - bans;
banns of matrimony.

bans - see banns.

bap. - baptized (q.v.).

baptisata; baptisatus (L) -
baptized.

baptisma; baptisus (L) -
baptism.

baptized - having had the
rite of baptism. Abbr. -
*ba.; bap.; bapt.; *bp.

baptizo (L) - baptize.

barbatus (L) - bearded;
adult.

barn (D) (No) (Sw) - child.

barnebarn (D) - grandchild.

barne-barn (No) - grand-
child.

barne-barnsbarn (No) -
great-grandchild.

barne-barns gutt (No) -
great-grandson.

barne-barns pike (No) -
great-granddaughter.

barnlös (Sw) - childless.

barnløs (D) childless.

baron - orig., one of a class of tenants in chief of the king or other feudal superior holding by military or other honorable service. Later, baron became restricted to the King's barons who were summoned to the council by writ; a nobleman. Heraldry, a husband as, baron and feme - husband and wife. (see feudal system).

Bartholomeus (L) - Bartholomew.

Base (G) - cousin.

baseborn - of low parentage; born out of wedlock.

bastard - a "natural" child; a child begotten and born out of wedlock.

battesaro (It) - baptized.

battesimo (It) - baptism.

Balt.; *Balto. - Baltimore.

Baudwinus (L) - Baldwin.

bäuerlich (G) - peasantlike.

bautizado (Sp) - baptized.

B.C. - before Christ (67 B. C. = 67 years before Christ).

B.C. - British Columbia.

bcer. - *birthcertificate.

bd. - *birthdate.

B.⸝du⸝Rh. (Fr) - Bouches⸝ du⸝Rhône.

bearing - (usually plural) any single emblem or charge in an escutcheon or coat of arms (qq.v.).

Bearrokscira (L) - Berkshire.

Beatricia, Beatrix (L) - Beatrice.

bedaget (D) - aged.

Beddeford (L) - Bedfordshire.

Bedeforda (L) - Bedford.

Bedfordia (L) - Bedford.

Beds. (E) - Bedford.

bedstefader (D) - grandfather.

bedstemofer (D) - grandmother.

bedyddiwyd (W) - baptized.

bef. - *before.

begraven (Du) (G) - buried.

begravet (D) (No) - buried.

bejaard, oud (Du) - aged, old.

Belg. - Belgium.

ben (Heb) - son.

bene quiescat (L) - may he rest well. Abbr. - b.q.

benyw (W) - woman (in So. Wales).

bequest - act of bequeathing, or leaving by will; also, that which is left by will.

Berceia (L) - Berkshire.

Bercheria (L) - Berkshire.

Berkeia (L) - Berkshire.

Berkeria (L) - Berkshire.

Berks. (E) - Berkshire.

beste-far (No) - grandfather.

beste-foreldre (No) - grandfather and grandmother, grandparents.

bestemor (No) - grand-

# GENEALOGICAL DICTIONARY      149

mother.

bet. - *between.

bet-overgrootvader (Du) - 2nd great-grandfather.

bet-over-overgrootvader (Du) - 3rd great-grandfather.

bet-over-over-overgrootvader (Du) - 4th great-grandfather.

bezirk (Sz) - county.

B'ham - *Birmingham.

bibliography - the description of books and manuscripts, with the notices of editions, dates of printing, etc.

biennium - a period of two years.

bill of sale - a formal instrument for the conveyance or transfer of title to goods and chattels.

biography - the written history of a person's life.

bis - a duplicate; repitition; a replica.

bis (L) - twice; in a twofold manner.

bisabuela (Sp) - great-grandmother.

bisabuelo (Sp) - great-grandfather.

bisava (It) - great-grandmother.

bisavo (It) - great-grandfather.

biskopsstift - see stift.

bisnieta (Sp) - great-granddaughter.

bisnieto (Sp) - great-grand-

son.

Blestium (L) - Monmouth.

blwyddyn (W) - year.

bndsmn. - *bondsman (q.v.)

bo. - *born; *bought; *bottom.

bona fied - in good faith; without fraud.

bondsman - a slave; villein; serf; a surety on a bond; one who is bound for another. Abbr. *bndsnm.

bonedd (W) - pedigree.

bonus (L) - good; kind; high; honourable.

Borg. (Ic) - Borgarfjardarsysla.

Bornhm. (D) - Bornholm.

borough - among the Anglo-Saxons, the enclosure protecting a house; a fortified house; a fortified group of houses; later; a town, or urban constituency sharing in the election of a member or members to Parliament.

b.o.t.p. - both of this parrish.

bounty land warrant - a right granted for military service involving a specific number of acres of unallocated public land. (ABC p. 75; SR p. 19).

bovate - an obsolete English unit of land measure, varying from 7 to 32 acres.

Boyd's Marriage Index - an index to many of the early

marriages of England.

bp. - *baptized (q.v.).

bpl. - place of birth.

b.q. - bene quiescat (q.v.).

Br. - British.

br.; bro; - brother (q.v.).

Brabant. (Bel) - Brabant.

brand - a mark of identification burned into the flank or side of an animal to show ownership. Brands have been registered for many years and may assist genealogists as they were very often hereditary. See earmark.

Brandbg. (G) - Brandenburg.

brawd (W) - brother.

B.∕Rhin (Fr) - Bas∕Rhin.

Brigida, Brigitta (L) - Bridget.

Brit. - British, Britian.

bro. - brother.

bro (W) - country

broder, bror (D) - brother.

broder (Sw) - brother.

broderdatter (D) - brother's daughter (niece).

brodersøn (D) - brother's son (nephew).

broeder (Du) - brother.

bro-i-l; bro-il.; bro. il. - *brother-in-law (q.v.).

bror (No) - brother.

brorsdotter (Sw) - brother's daughter (niece).

brorson (Sw) - brother's son (nephew).

brother - son of your father & mother; one of a common family; in a more general sense, a fellow man. Abbr. - b.; br.; bro (see SYA p. 140 for instability of use).

brother-in-law - husband of your wife's sister; husband of your sister. Abbr. - *bro-i-l.; *bro. il.; *bro.-i-l. (See SYA p. 140).

bruder (G) - brother.

Brunsw. (G) - Brunswick (Braunschweig).

Bses∕Alpes (Fr) - Basses∕Alpes.

Bses∕Pyr. (Fr) - Basses∕Pyrenees.

Bu. - Abu (q.v.).

Buckingeham (L) - Buckinghamshire.

Buckinghamia (L) - Buckingham.

Bucks. (E) - Buckingham.

Budiforda (L) - Bedford.

buitenechelijk (Du) - illegitimate.

bur. - *buried.

burg (G) - castle.

Burgenld. (Aus) - Burgenland.

burgher registers - registers maintained as proof of citizenship in a given town in Switzerland. (GGR p. 262).

Buskd. (No) - Buskerud.

bustum (L) - tomb, sepulchral.

by (D) - city, town.

by (No) - small town, village.

## C

c.; ca.; circa. - about (or around a certain year.)

ca. - circa (q.v.).

cadastral survey, map, or plan - a survey, map or plan for making a cadastre. Usually made on a large scale, about a square inch to the acre.

cadastre (er) - an official register of real estate, used in apportioning taxes.

cadaver (L) - dead body; corpse.

cadet (Fr) - youngest.

cado (L) - to be slain; to abate; to decay; to end; to fail.

Caecilia (L) - Cecily.

Caecilius (L) - Cecil.

caedes (L) - slaughter; murder; persons slain or murdered.

caelebs, coelebs (L) - unmarried.

Caerns. (W) - Caernarvon.

Caith. (Sc) - Caithness.

Caius (L) - Kay.

Cajun - corruption of Arcadian; in La. descendant of an Arcadian.

calendar, Old Style - see Julian calendar; double dating.

calends - the first day of the Roman month; a calendar; a record; a register.

Calif. - California.

call number - the number assigned a book in a library, used when calling or asking for the same.

calo (L) - soldier's boy; low servant.

Camboricum, Camborium (L) - Cambridge.

Cambs. (E) - Cambridge.

canon - a decree, decision, regulation, code or constitution made by ecclesiastical authority; a law, or rule of doctrine or discipline, enacted by a council and confirmed by the Pope or the sovereign.

Cantabrigia (L) - Cambridgeshire.

Cantia, Cantium (L) - Kent.

canton - a small territorial division of a country; one of the states of the Swiss Confederation; a rectangular division of the shield, used in modern heraldry for the diminutive of the old quarter.

canton (Fr) - county in Switzerland; sub-division of an arrondissement. (in Belgium a district under the jurisdiction of a Judge of Peace).

canus (L) - hoary, gray; foamy; old age.

caput (L) - head; source;

life; person; intelligence; chief.

card catalogue - a catalogue, list or index of the books and other material of a library entered on cards. Most genealogical libraries have a surname catalogue and a place or geographical catalogue. Also-card index.

Cards. (W) - Cardigan.

Carms. (W) - Carmarthen.

Carolus (L) - Charles.

casado (Sp) - married.

cath. - catherdral (q.v.).

cathedral - the principal church of a diocese. Abbr. - cath.

causidicus (L) - barrister; advocate.

C⁄du⁄N. (Fr) - Côtes du⁄ Nord.

cefn der (W) - male cousin.

célibataire (Fr) - unmarried.

cem. - *cemetery

cen. - *census.

censeo (L) - to count; to reckon; to tax, to vote.

census - a official enumeration of the population of a country, city or other administrative district, with statistics of commerce, wealth and social conditions; a tax, esp. a poll tax.

census records or returns - the records compiled by the census takers and kept mostly by the Bureau of Census.

census (L) - valuation of every Roman Citizen's estate; mustering of the people.

cer. - *certificate.

cerca de (Sp) - about.

Cernualia, Curnualia (L) - Cornwall.

certified copy - a copy made or attest by officers having charge of the original and authorized to give copies.

certified extract - in genealogy, a certified copy of parts of a document, such as a will, giving only the information pertaining to relationships, locations, etc.

Cestria (L) - Chester.

Cestrisria (L) - Cheshire.

cf., confer; (L) - compare.

ch. - church; child; children; chief.

ch(s). - church(es).

chapelry - the territorial district assigned to a chapel; the chapel with all its apurtenances (records, etc.) (see GGR p. 223).

charge (Her) - to place a bearing on a shield, etc.

Char⁄Marit. (Fr) - Char⁄ ente⁄Maritime.

checky (Her) - checked or checkered; of a field or charge - divided into rectangles of alternate tinctures.

Ches. (E) – Cheshire.

Chestria, Chestrum (L) – Chester.

ch/o – *child of.

chr. – christened (q.v.).

chris. – *christened.

Christened – to receive or initate into the visible church of Christ by baptism; to baptize; to name at baptism; to give a name to.

Christopherus (L) –Christopher.

churching(e)s – administration or reception of a rite by which one is churched; specif., a ceremony by which, after childbirth, women are received in the church with prayers, blessings and thanksgiving.

churchyard – the yard or enclosure belonging to a church part of which is often used as a burial ground; God's acre.

chwaer (W) – sister.

cir. – circa; circum (qq.v.).

circ. – circa; circum (qq.v).

circa (L) – about; near to. Abbr. – c.; ca.; cir.; circ.

circiter; circum (L) – about; near; towards. Abbr. – c.; cir.; circ.

città (It) – city, town.

city – a large important town; U.S.; an incorporated municipality; Canada: a municipality of high rank, usually based on population; British: a borough, usually the seat of a bishop, upon which the dignity of the title has been conferred by the Crown.

ciudad (Sp) – city, town.

ciuitate (L) – city.

civicus (L) – civic; civil; pertaining to the Roman state.

civil law – the laws of a state or nation regulating ordinary private matters (distinguished from criminal, military, or political matters); the body of law proper to the city or state of Rome, as distinct from that common to all nations; the systems of law derived from Roman law (distinguished from common law, cannon law).

Clack. (Sc) –Clackmannan.

claddwyd (W) – buried.

clan – a group of people of common descent.

Claudia, Claudia Castra (L) – Gloucester.

Claudiana provincia (L) – Gloucestershire.

Claudiocestria (L) – Gloucester.

Cleocestria (L) – Gloucester.

Clevum (L) - Gloucester.

cloister; cloyster (L) - a monastery or convent.

co. - county (q.v.); Company.

coat of arms - a surcoat or tabard embroidered with heraldic devices, worn by medieval knights over their armor; the heraldic bearings of a person; the hatchment; an escutcheon. (GGR 217-223).

codicil - a supplement to a will, modifying, adding to or changing it; In Roman, canon and early English law a kind of informal will made without the appointment of executors said to be essential to a formal will.

coelebs (L) - single.

cognate - related by birth; of the same parentage, descent, etc.; related on the mother's side.

cognatus (L) - related by birth; kinsman; kinswoman.

cognomen (L) - family name; epithet; the Roman name corresponding to our surname.

c.o.h.; coh. - *coheir (q.v.).

coheir; coheiress - a joint heir. Abbr. - *coh.; c.o.h.

col. - colony; colonel.

coll. - college; collections.

collateral ancestors - belonging to the same ancestral stock but not in direct line of descent; opposed to lineal; father and son are lineal, uncles, aunts, cousins, etc., are collateral kinsman.

collateral lines - persons descending from collateral kinsman.

College of Arms - Heralds' College (q.v.).

College of Heralds - Heralds' College (q.v.).

Colo. - Colorado.

colona (L) - country woman.

colonus (L) - husbandman, farmer.

com. - *comitatus; *county (qq.v.); commissioner; commander; commentary; committee; common; commoner; communicate.

comitatus (L) - English county; escort; train, retinue; company; troop. Abbr. - *com.

common law - a system of law originating in England, as distinct from the civil or Roman Law and the canon or ecclesiastical law; the unwritten law.

common-law-marriage - a marriage without ceremony, civil or ecclesiastical. Recognized at times in some places, mostly unrecognized.

commoner - a citizen or burgess; one of a town council; one of the common people, having no rank of nobility.

communicant - one who partakes of, or is entitled to partake of, the sacrament of the Lord's Supper; a church member

comp. - *company.

compar (L) - alike, equal; comrade; lover, consort.

compt (L) - county.

comté (Fr) - county.

con. - conjunx (q.v.).

condado (Sp) - county.

condito (L) - condition; situation; agreement; marriage; married person.

confirmation - in various churches: a rite supplemental to baptism.

coniugal (It) - married.

conjugium (L) - marriage; wedlock; husband.

conjunx (L) - wife. Abbr. - con.

conjux (L) - spouse; wife; bride; husband.

Conn. - Connecticut.

consanguineus (L) - related by blood; brotherly; sisterly.

consanguinity - state of being related by blood, or descended from a common ancestor.

consobrina (L) - first cousin on the father's side.

consobrinus (L) - (female)

cousin-german (on the mother's side).

consort - a partner, companion, or collegue; a wife or husband; spouse; mate. (SYA 79).

Constantia (L) - Constance.

cont. - continued; contract.

contea (It) - county.

contemporary records - records written or compiled at the time the event occured; records originating or recorded in the same period.

contr. -*contrast; contract

Cophgn. (D) - Copenhagen.

copulerede (D) - married.

Corinea (L) - Cornwall.

Corn. (E) - Cornwall. Cornish.

Cornuallia, Cornubia (L) - Cornwall.

corp. - corporal.

corpus (L) body, substance; flesh; corpse.

Cos. - Counties.

couns. - *counsellor.

county - an earldom; the domain of a count or earl. In Great Britain and Northern Ireland one of the territorial divisions constituting the chief units for administrative, judicial and political purposes. The first districts to be called counties were the old Anglo Saxon shires, often called the ancient, or geographical counties, or, more commonly, counties at large, which had various historical origins going back to Anglo-Saxon days. Later the term was applied to: 1. Certain districts consisting of towns or cities with neighboring territory separated out of the older shires and given the organization of counties (and called counties corporate or corporate counties). 2. Certain duchies (as Cornwall, Shetland, etc.). 3. Administrative divisions (often not coincident with the older counties) to which the administrative functions (but not the judicial or political ones) of the older counties have been transferred under the Local Government Act of 1888 and which are called administrative counties. In Scotland, the 33 civil counties into which the country is divided, is substantially the same as that of England. In the U.S., it is the largest division of local government in all the states except Louisiana, where the corresponding division is the parish. Abbr. - Co.; co.; ct.; Latin - *com.

county palatine - dominion or territory of a count or earl palatine. In England, county of which the earl or count had originally royal powers with exclusive civil and criminal jurisdiction. (now abolished.)

county town - an English town which is the seat of county administration.

court docket - see trial docket.

cous. - *cousin (q.v.).

cous-i-l. - cousin-in-law (q.v.).

cousin - anyone collaterally related more remotely than a brother or sister; a son or daughter of one's own uncle or aunt (called more fully own, first, or full cousin, or cousin-german);paternal cousin - on the father's side; maternal cousin - on the mother's side. (see relationship chart for detailed cousin relationship) Cousin is sometimes used in a general sense as a sort of title of endearment even when there is no blood relationship. Abbr. - *cous.

cousin; cousine (Fr) - cousin.

cousin-german - first cousin; a son or daughter of your father's or mother's brother or sister.

cousin-in-law - one married to a cousin. Abbr. - *cous-i-l.

C.P. - Cape of Good Hope, know as Cape Province. (So. Africa).

C.R. - *church record.

crest - a bearing or device set not upon the shield but on the helm, and used separately as an ornament or cognizance for plate, liveries, and the like. (see bearings, shield, coat of arms, arms).

croft - a small agriculture holding worked by a peasant.

crofter - on who rents or tills a croft (q.v.).

crspd. - *correspond; *correspondence.

csn. - *cousin; *cousins.

ct. - court; county.

cuadro genealógico (Sp) - pedigree chart.

cuis susceptores (L) - godparents.

cugina (It) - female cousin.

cugino (It) - male cousin.

cugino germano (It) - first cousin.

cum (L) - with; along with; under; in; by.

Cumb. (E) - Cumberland.

Cumberlandia, Cumbria (L) - Cumberland.

curate - one who is a deputy of a rector or

vicar (qq.v.).

Curnualia (L) - Cornwall.

CW. - *Civil War.

cyfnither (W) - female cousin.

cyndad (W) - ancestor.

C.Z. - Territory of Canal Zone.

## D

D. - Dutch.

d. - date; daughter (q.v.); day; days; dead; died; *death.

da. - daughter (q.v.); day; days.

dag (D) (Du) (No) (Sw) day

Dal. (Ir) - Dalasysla.

Damnonia (L) - Devonshire.

Dan. - Danish; Denmark (Danmark).

D. & C. - Dean and Chapter (q.v.).

d & coh. - *daughter and coheiress (q.v.).

d. & h. - *daughter and heiress (q.v.).

D&W. - *Deed & Wills.

dans l'enfance (Fr) - infant.

D.A.R. - Daughters of the American Revolution (q.v.).

Darbia (L) - Derby.

dates, double - see double-dating.

dator (L) - giver.

datter (D) (No) - daughter.

datterdatter (D) - daughter's daughter (granddaughter).

datter-datter (No) - daughter's daughter (granddaughter).

Dattersøn (D) - daughter's son (grandson).

datter-sønn (No) - daughter's son (grandson).

dau. - daughter (q.v.).

daughter - one's female child; also used as a title of endearment for any female, whether there be blood relationship or not. Abbr. - d.; da.; dau.; *daugr.; *dt. (see SYA p. 140).

daughter-in-law - the wife of one's son. Abbr. dau-i-l. (see SYA p. 140).

Daughters of the American Revolution - a patriotic society of American women, organized to preserve the memory of those active in achieving American independence. Abbr. D.A.R.

Daughters of the Revolution - a patriotic society of woman, similar to D.A.R. Abbr. - D.R.

daugr. - *daughter (q.v.).

dau-i-l - *daughter-in-law (q.v.).

daus. - daughters.

D.B. - *Domesday Book (q.v.).

D.C. - Dist of Columbia.

de (L) - down from; from; out of; about; at; for; etc.

dea. - deacon.

deac. - * deacon.

dean - a chief or head of ten men; hence, a tithingman; a head over ten monks in a monastery; the head of the chapter, or body of canons or prebendaries. (see Dean and Chapter).

Dean and Chapter - Constitutes the legal corporation of the church. The dean is the head of the chapter which is a regular assembly of the canons of a cathedral or a collegiate church, or of the members of other religious orders. Abbr. - D. and C.

deanery - the office, position of official residence of the dean; a subdivision of an archdeaconry. Also Rural Deanery. Several parishes make a deanery.

death notice - in some countries, the notice of death filed with the probate court with or without a will, giving considerable genealogical information.

dec.; decd; dec'd. - deceased.

décédé, décédée (Fr) - died

décédé sans posterité (Fr) - died without issue.

decedent - a deceased person.

decessit sine prole (L) - he

died without issue. Abbr. - d.s.p.

decessit vita matris (L) - he died in his mother's lifetime. Abbr. -*d.v.m.

decessit vita patris (L) - he died in his father's lifetime. Abbr. - d.v.p.

decido (L) - to fall down; to die.

Declaration of Intention - a sworn statement by an alien that he intends to become a citizen.

deed of indenture - see indenture.

deed - a sealed instrument in writing, on paper or parchment, duly executed and delivered, containing some transfer, bargain, or contract; also loosely, such an instrument before it has been given effect by delivery. In its broadest sense deed properly included every such instrument; but it is often used specifically of an instrument conveying a fee of land, as distinguished from a mortgage, lease or other instruments under seal. A will although under seal is not a deed, because not delivered and accepted.

defunct - dead.

degener (L) - degenerate; lowborn; base.

Del. - Delaware.

De La, De Le, Del (Norman Fr)- all mean "from the" followed by a place.

Den. - Denmark.

Dena Victrix (L) - Chester.

Denb. (W) - Denbigh.

denizen - an inhabitant; an alien admitted to residence.

denomino (L) - to name; to call.

denicalis (L) - solemn purification of a house, on the tenth day after the death of a person.

denubo (L) - to marry; to marry beneath one's condition.

Deorbeia (L) - Derby.

department (Fr) - county or province in France.

depose - say under oath; testify.

deposition - a testifying or testimony taken down in writing under oath of affirmation in reply to interrogatories, before a competent officer to replace the viva voce (oral) testimony of the witness.

Derby. (E) - Derbyshire.

Derebiscira (L) - Derbyshire.

Derry (Ire) - Londonderry.

desc. - descendant (q.v.).

descendant - one who descends, as an offspring, however remotely; opposed to ancestor, ascendent. Abbr. - desc.

Deutsch (G) - German.

Deuna (L) - Chester.

Deva, Devana, Devania (L) - Chester.

devisee - a person to whom lands or other real property are devised or given by will.

devisor - a giver of lands or real estate by will; a testator.

Devon. (E) - Devonshire.

Devonia (L) - Devonshire.

dft - defendant.

dí (It) - day.

dia (Sp) - day.

dibriod (W) - unmarried.

dico (L) - to tell; to order; to call; to plead; etc.

die (L) - see dies.

died without issue - died without having children.

dies (L) - day; daylight; day of burial. Abbr. - d.

dinas (W) - city.

dio. - *diocese (q.v.).

diocése (Fr) - bishopric, presided over by a bishop

diocese - the administrative division of a country; esp., a division of the prefecture of the Roman Empire; the circuit or extent of a bishop's jurisdiction; the district in which a bishop has authority. Abbr. - *dio.

discidium (L) separation; divorce.

disinherit - to cut off from,

or deprive of, an inheritance or hereditary succession.

dist. - district.

distribution - the apportionment, by a court, of the personal property of an intestate among those entitled to it.

District Land Office Plat Book - books or rather maps which show the location of the land of the patentee. (see patent; also ABC p. 76).

District Land Office Tract Books - books which list individaul entries by range and township. (ABC p. 76).

div. - divorced.

Divana (L) - Chester.

diwrnod (W) - day.

do. - ditto; the same.

d/o - *daughter of.

døbt (D) - baptized.

doc. - document; doctor.

dochter (Du) - daughter.

document - an original or official paper relied upon as the basis, proof or support of anything.

documented history - a history which has as its basis documents, such as certified, photostat or originals copied verbatim (see legal and historical methods).

død (D) - died.

døde (No) - died.

døde barnløs (No) - died without issue.

døduden afkom (D) - died without issue.

död utan bröstarvinge (Sw) - died without issue.

dom. - domestic.

Domesday Book - the ancient record of the Grand, or Great Inquest or Survey of the lands of England, made 1085-86 by order of William the Conqueror. It consists of two volumes sometimes called the Little Domesday and the Great Domesday. The Domesday Book gives a census-like description of the realm, with the names of the proprietors, the nature, extent value, liabilities, etc., of their properties. Abbr. - *D.B.

domina (L) - mistress of a family; lady; wife.

dominus (L) - master of the house; owner; ruler; "Sir".

Domnania (L) - Devonshire.

domsaga (Sw) - judicial district or circuit.

domus (L) - house; home; family; native country; temple.

donation application - application for frontier land in Florida, New Mexico, Oregon or Washington. Given to an actual set-

tler upon certain conditions. (see ABC p. 75; SR p. 19).

donation lands - see donation application.

donee - one to whom a gift is made.

donor - a person who makes a gift.

dópt (Sw) - baptized.

Dorbeia (L) - Derby.

Dorcestria (L) - Dorsetshire.

dorf (G) (Sz) - village.

Dorothea (L) - Dorothy.

dorp (Ne) - village.

Dorset. (E) - Dorsetshire.

Dorsetania, Dorsetia (L) - Dorsetshire.

dött (Sw) - died.

dotter (Sw) - daughter.

dotterdotter (Sw) - daughter's daughter (granddaughter).

dotterson (Sw) - daughter's son (grandson).

double-dating - a system of double-dating was used in England and America from 1582 to 1752 because it was not clear as to whether the year commenced on Jan. 1 or March 25. The new Gregorian Calendar (q.v.) year started Jan. 1 and the old Julian (q.v.) year started on March 25. Double-dating is very common during the years 1582 to Sept. 2, 1752 but was only necessary from Jan. 1 to March 24 of each year. During this period most dates were written similar to this: 25 Jan. 1744/5, indicating that the year was 1744 by the old style or Julian Calendar and 1745 by the new style or Gregorian Calendar. However, some of the churches did not recognize the new style and care must be used in figuring dates of this period. From March 25 to Dec. 31 the year was the same on both calendars so no double dates were necessary. (see G GR pp. 320-330; ABC p. 90; 1953 HB p. 220).

dower - that portion of, or interest in, the real estate of a deceased husband which the law gives to his widow during her life; the property which a woman brings to a husband in marriage - now usually called dowery.

døpt (No) - baptized.

dpl. - *place of death.

D. R. - Daughters of the Revolution (q.v.).

dragoon - ancient carbine; dragon; a mounted infantryman armed with a dragoon.

dreng, drengebarn (D) -

boy, male child.

Drente. (Ne) - Drenthe.

d.s. - document signed.

dsct. - *descendant.

D. / Sevres (Fr) - Deux/ Sevres.

d.s.p. - decessit sine prole (q.v.).

dt. - *daughter (q.v.).

Du. - Dutch.

duco (L) - to marry; to take; to bring; to persuade; etc.

Dumf. (Sc) - Dumfries.

Dumnonia (L) -Devonshire.

Dunb. (Sc) - Dunbarton.

Dunholmus, Dunholmum (L) - Durham.

Duria (L) - Dorsetshire.

dux (L) - leader; guide.

duxit (L) - married; husband.

d.v.m. - * decessit vita matris (q.v.).

d.v.p. - decessit vita patris (q.v.).

dwt. - pennyweight(s).

d.y. - *died young.

dydd (W) - day.

dyn (W) - man.

dynes (W) - woman.

E

e. - east or eastern.

ead. - *eadem (q.v.).

eadem (L) - in the same way. Abbr. - *ead.

Eadmundus (L) - Edmund.

Eadwardus (L) - Edward.

earl - among the Anglo-

# GENEALOGICAL DICTIONARY 163

Saxons, a warrior, esp. one of noble rank; a man; the viceroy of one of the four great divisions of England; a nobleman ranking below a marquis, and above a viscount.

earmark – a mark of identification on the ear of an animal, usually used in connection with a brand to identify ownership. Earmarks and brands (q.v.) were registered and sometimes assist genealogists as they were quite often passed from father to son.

East-Sexena (L) – Essex.

Eboracum (L) – York.

Ebor'scira (L) – Yorkshire.

Eburacum (L) – York.

ecclesia (L) – church.

echtgenoot (Du) – husband.

echtgenote (Du) – wife.

ed. – edited; edition; editor.

edad (Sp) – age.

Editha (L) – Edith.

editicius (L) – named; allowed.

educ. – education or educated.

E./er/L. (Fr) – Eure/et/Loir.

E. Fland. (Bel) – Oost Vlaanderen.

e.g. – exempli gratia (L. for example).

Egidius (L) – Giles.

ego (L) – I; I myself; house; family.

ehefrau (G) – wife.

ehemann (G) – husband.

ei ferch (W) – daughter, his daughter.

Einwohner-Meldeamt (Sz) (G) – citizen's registration office.

ej. – *ejus (q.v.).

ejus (L) – his; hers; of him; (filius ejus – son of him; uxur ejus – wife of him). Abbr. – *ej.

Eleanora (L) – Eleanor.

Elena (L) – Ellen.

Elisabetha (L) – Elizabeth, Isabella.

el mayor (Sp) – eldest.

el menor (Sp) – youngest.

E. Lothian (Sc) – East Lothian.

elst (No) – eldest.

elugeo (L) – to mourn the full time.

Emelina (L) – Emily.

emigrant – one departing from a country to settle permanently elsewhere. (see immigrant).

emigration records – the records made of persons leaving a country (see GGR pp. 34-37).

emorior (L) – to die; to perish; to cease.

en bas âge (Fr) – infant.

enfant (Fr) – child.

Eng. – England; English.

enke (D) (No) – widow.

enkel (G) – grandson.

enkelin (G) – granddaughter.

enkemand (D) – widower.

enkemann (No) - widower.

eno. - *enough.

Ens. - Ensign.

enseveli, ensevelie (Fr) - buried.

enteré, enterrée (Fr) - buried.

enterrado (Sp) - buried.

entry - the act of making or entering a record; that which is entered.

enubo (L) - to marry out of one's rank; to marry and leave the paternal house.

enumeration - a census (q.v.).

enumerator - one who counts or lists; the census taker.

enuptio (L) - marrying out of one's rank.

enutrio (L) - to nourish; to bring up.

eo (L) - thither; so far; to go; to walk; there; etc.

eodem (L) - to the same place or purpose.

eodem die - same day

Ep. - Episcopus (q.v.).

Episcopus (L) - bishop. Abbr. - Ep.; Epus.

epitaph - an inscription on or at a tomb or grave in memory of the one buried there.

epitaphium (L) - funeral oration.

épouse (Fr) - wife.

époux (Fr) - husband.

E. Pruss. (G) - Ostpreussen.

Epus. - Episcopus (q.v.).

ergo (L) - wherefore; therefore; then; now.

erratum (L) - error, mistake. (pl. errata).

escutcheon - the variously shaped surface, usually a shield, on which armorial bearings are depicted, marshaled and displayed. (see GGR p. 217; also heraldry).

esi-isä (Fi) - ancestor.

esikoinen (Fi) - firstborn.

esposa (Sp) - wife.

esposo (Sp) - husband.

Essexa (L) - Essex.

est. - *estate; *established

estates in litigation - estates left with no apparent heir or with no will and going through the judicial process to determine who shall inherit.

estd. - *estimated.

Estsexa (L) - Essex.

et (L) - and; also; yet; etc.

et.al. (L) - et alibi or et alli; and others; and elsewhere. (Look for others).

éta (It) - age.

et seq.; et seqq. (L) - et sequentes, et sequentia; and those that follow.

et ux. - et uxor (q.v.).

et uxor (L) - and wife. Abbr. - et ux.

Everwyk (L) - York.

evidence - that which is submitted as a means of ascertaining the truth of any alleged matter of fact. It may be done by means of witnesses, records, documents, concrete objects, etc., and may be for the purpose of proving or disproving any matter.

evito (L) - to kill.

ewyllys, ewyllys diweddaf (W) - will, testament.

ewyrth, ewyythr (W) - uncle

ex asse heres (L) - universal or sole heir.

exc. - except; excellency; excepted; exchange.

excerpt - an extract; a passage selected or copied from a book or record.

excessus (L) - departure; death.

Exchequer Rolls - financial account of various sheriffs and their assistants, who collected rents and fines in Great Britain (see GGR p. 261).

excise - any duty, toll or tax; to lay or impose an excise upon.

exciseman - an officer who inspects and rates articles liable to excise duty.

ex, e (before consonants) (L) - out of; from; down from; after, etc.

exec. - executor (q.v.).

executor - the person appointed by a testator to execute his will, or to see its provisions carried into effect, after his decease; the personal representative of the testator (q. v.). Abbr. - exec.; *exec.; exors.

executrix - a woman exercising the functions of an executor. Abbr. - *exox.

exeo (L) - to go out or away; to escape; to end; to die.

Exexa (L) - Essex.

exhalo (L) - to breath out; to evaporate; to die.

exheres (L) - disinherited; disinherited person.

exor. - *executor (q.v.).

exorior (L) - to arise; to begin; to originate.

exors - *executors (q.v.).

exox. - *executrix (q.v.).

exr. - executor (q.v.).

exrx. - excutrix (q.v.).

exscribo (L) - to write off; to copy.

exsequialis (L) - funeral.

exspiro (L) - to breath out; to exhale; to cease; to die.

extract - a selection from a writing; a quotation. (see certified extract.)

extra-parochal district - special district with certain independent jurisdictions in England.

exx. - executrix (q.v.).

eyf. (Ir) - Eyjafardarsyla.

# F

f. - father (q.v.); feast; feet; feminine; form; folio; following; foot; for; etc.

faber (L) - artisan; workman; smith; carpenter.

fabricator (L) - artificer; farmer; contriver.

facsimile - an exact and detailed copy of anything.

faddere (D) - witnesses.

fader (Sw) - father.

fader, far (D) - father.

Faero. (D) - Faerøerne.

falleció (Sp) - died.

fam. - family or families.

familia (L) - family; servants or slaves belonging to one master; household; sect.

famula (L) - female slave; maid-servant.

famulus (L) - slave, servant; attendant.

fanciullo (It) - child.

far (No) - father.

farbroder (D) - father's brother (uncle).

farbror (Sw) -father's brother (uncle).

farfar (D) (No) (Sw) - father's father (grandfather).

farfars far (Sw) -father's father's father (great-grandfather).

farfars mor (Sw) -father's father's mother (great-grandmother).

farmor (D) (No) (Sw) - father's mother (grandmother).

farmors far (Sw) -father's mother's father (great-grandfather).

farmors mor (Sw) - father's mother's mother (great-grandmother).

fars farbror (Sw) -father's father's brother (granduncle).

fars faster (Sw) - father's father's sister (grandaunt).

fars morbror (Sw) - father's mother's brother (granduncle).

fars moster (Sw) -father's mother's sister (grandaunt).

farsøster (D) - father's sister (aunt).

F.A.S.G. - Fellow American Society of Genealogists.

faster (D) - maternal aunt.

faster (Sw) - father's sister (aunt).

father - the nearest male ancestor; any male ancestor; a title of endearment bestowed upon an older, close associate with no blood relationship; a dignitary of the church. Abbr. - f.

father-i-l -*father-in-law.

father-in-law - father of your wife or husband. Abbr. - *father-i-l.

fätter (D) - male cousin.

f.e. - for example.

feast days - a holy day set apart annually for solemn commemoration. In the middle Ages and later many records established their dates from various feast days, some fixed and some movable. (see GGR p 320).

fecerunt (L) - they did it. Abbr. - ff.

fee - an estate of inheritance in land, being either a fee simple or a fee tail (qq.v.); an estate in land held of a feudal lord on condition of the performing of certain services.

fee simple - a fee (q.v.) without limitation to any particular class of heirs or restrictions upon alienation.

fee tail - an estate of inheritance or fee (q.v.) limited to lineal descendant heirs (or heirs of the body) of the person to whom it is granted.

feet of fines - began with the reign of Richard I, of England and were practically deeds transferring land, though nominally the "finis" or end of a fictitious suit; they are of great value to the genealogist, giving mi-nute accounts of land transfers at a date when deeds were exceedingly rare. (see GGR p. 230).

femina (L) - female, woman; she.......

femme (Fr) - wife, woman.

femmina (It) - woman.

feod - feud (q.v.).

fere (L) - nearly; almost; about; very; in general.

Fermanh. (Ire) - Fermanagh.

ferrarius (L) - Ironmonger; relating to or belonging to iron.

Ferulega (L) - Hereford.

fetter (No) - male cousin.

feud - an estate of land held of a feudal lord on condition of the performing of certain services; a territory held in in fee (q.v.).

feudal system - the system of polity which prevailed in Europe in the Middle Ages, based upon the relation of lord to vassal, with the holding of the land in feud, fief or fee (qq.v.) (baron).

FF. - Frates (q.v.).

ff. - fecerunt (q.v.); following (pages); ff is also used in Old English script as a capitol "F".

F.F.V. - First Families of Virginia.

f.i. - for instance.

F.I.A.G. - Fellow Institute

of American Genealogy (defunct).

fid. - fiduciary (q.v.)

fiduciary - a person to whom property is entrusted to hold, control, or manage for another. Abbr. - fid.

fief - a feudal estate; a fee; a feud (qq.v.).

figlia (It) - daughter.

figlio (It) - son

f-i-l - *father-in-law.

filia (L) - daughter; female offspring.

filia fratris (L) - brother's daughter (niece).

filia sororis (L) - sister's daughter (niece).

filiola (L) - little daughter.

filiolus (L) - little son.

filius (L) - son; male offspring.

filius fratris (L) - brother's son; nephew.

filius sororis (L) - sister's son; nephew.

fille (Fr) - daughter, girl.

fils (Fr) - son.

Finist. (Fr) - Finestère.

Finmk. (No) - Finnmark.

fistulator (L) - piper; one who plays on a reed-pipe.

Fitz (Norman Fr) - a prefix to the father's name, meaning son.

fixed feast days - see feast days.

fl. - floruit (q.v.).

Fla - Florida.

flicka (Sw) - girl.

Flints (W) - Flintshire.

floruit (L) - he flourished. Abbr. - fl.

född (Sw) - born.

født (D) (No) - born.

fol. - following.

foraeldre (D) - parents.

forfader (D) - forefather, ancestor.

förfader (Sw) - ancestor.

forsamling (Sw) - church parish.

församling (Sw) - firstborn.

førstefødt (D) firstborn, eldest.

fr. - frater (q.v.).

franc - or frei (G) - free.

Franciscus (L) - Francis.

Francus (L) - Frank.

frank - free; not in bondage; to exempt from charge from postage; to enable to pass or go freely or easily.

frank marriage - the tenure by which a man and his wife held an estate granted by a blood relative of the wife in consideration of their marriage (whether before or after it) to be held of the donor by the issue of the marriage to not less than the fourth generation and without other service than faithfulness to the grantor.

franklin - an English freeholder in the 14th & 15th centuries; a middle-class landowner.

Franklin, State of - the area once known as the "State of Franklin" was never officially recognized and was under consideration for only a short time. It is of importance to research in the southern states. Organized 1784 from the western part of North Carolina, ceased to exist 1788. (see ABC p 96).

Franks - members of the confederated German tribes who founded the Franklin Empire which eventually gave place to the medieval kingdoms that became France, Germany and Italy.

fratello (It) - brother.

frater (L) - brother; cousin; brother-in-law; kinsman. Abbr. - fr.

Fratres (L) - Brothers. Abbr. - FF.

fratricida (L) - murder of a brother.

fratris (L) - see frater.

fratris filia - see filia fratris.

frau (G) - woman.

fra will - below 40 pounds (sterling).

Fraxula Flu (L) - In Derbyshire.

Frdbg. (D) - Frederiksborg.

freehold - an estate in fee simple, in fee tail (qq.v.) of for life.

freeman - one who enjoys liberty, or who is not subject to the will of another; not a slave or vassal; one having the freedom of a company or municipality; (see SYA 141).

freeholder - the owner of a freehold.

frei (G) - free.

Freibg. (G) - Freiburg.

frère (Fr) - brother.

Friends - a religious sect with various divisions such as; Society of Friends, Religious Society of Friends, Orthodox Conservative Friends and Primative Friends. They are popularly called Quakers. The minutes of their Monthly Meetings (q.v.) furnish a wealth of genealogical information (see ABC p. 111).

Friesl. (Ne) - Friesland.

F.S.G. - Fellow Society of Genealogists, (British).

fuit (L) - was.

funebris (L) - funeral; deadly; mortal; cruel.

funereus (L) - funeral; deadly; destructive.

funero (L) - to kill. ruin; death.

furn. - *furniture.

fylker (No) - present term for county, shire.

## G

G. - German, Germany.

g. - grand; *great, (qq.v.).

Ga. - Georgia.

gaard (No) - farm or group of several farms.

gaardmand (D) - owner of house and ground, independent farmer.

Galfredus, Gaufridus (L) - Geoffrey.

Galterus (L) - Walter.

gammal (Sw) - old aged.

gammel (D) (No) old, aged.

ganwyd (W) - born.

G.A.R. - Grand Army of the Republic. An organization formed by veterans of the Union who fought in the Civil War.

garcon (Fr) - boy.

gard (Sw) - farm.

gardianus (L) church-warden.

gatte (G) - husband.

gattin (G) - wife.

Gavlebg. (Sw) - Gavleborg.

gazetteer - a geographical dictionary; a book giving names and descriptions of places in alphabetical order.

G.B. - Great Britain.

gch - *grandchildren.

gdn. - *guardian.

geboren (Du) (G) - born.

gedoopt (Du) - baptized.

geheiratet (G) - married.

gehucht (Ne) - hamlet.

gehuwd (Du) - married.

geld - a payment; a tax paid to the crown by landholders under Saxon and Norman kings.

Geld. (Ne) - Gelderland.

gemelli (L) - twin.

gemellus (L) - twin-born; twin.

geminus (L) - twin-born; double; both.

geneal. - genealogy (q.v.).

genealogia (It) (Sp) - pedigree.

genealogy - an account or history of the descent of a person, family or group from an ancestor or ancestors; the study of family pedigrees and the methods of investigation of them, regarded as a science or an art. Abbr. - geneal.

gener (L) - son-in-law; brother-in-law.

generation - a single step or stage in the succession of natural descent; a rank or remove in genealogy; the average lifetime of man, or the ordinary period of time at which one rank follows another, usually taken to be about 33 years.

genero (L) - to beget; bring to life.

generosi(sus) (L) - of noble birth.

generosos (L) - of noble birth; noble; generous;

brave.

geneth (W) - girl.

genetrix (L) - mother.

genialis (L) - pertaining to generation or birth; marry.

genitalis (L) - birth.

genitor (L) - begettor; father.

genitrix (L) - mother.

gens (L) -gentleman (q.v.).

gent. - gentleman.

gentilis (L) - of the same clan or race.

gentis (L) - gens (q.v.).

gentleman - a man well born; one of a good family though not noble; one entitled to bear a coat of arms; sometimes, any one above the social condition of a yeoman. (q. v.). Abbr - gent.

gentry - people of good breeding; gentlefolk; in England, those between the nobility and the yeomanry (q.v.).

genus (L) - birth; descent; origin; race; family.

Georgius (L) - George.

Ger. - German, Germany.

Gerardus (L) - Gerard.

germana (L) - sister.

germani (L) - borther.

germanus (L) -(of brothers and sisters), full; genuine, true.

geslachtsboom (Du) -pedigree.

gestorben (G) - died.

gestorven (Du) - died.

gestorven zonder nage-slacht (Du) - died without issue.

getauft (G) - baptized.

gf. - *grandfather.

gg. - great grand ,(q.v.).

ghost town - an abandoned town.

gift, gifte (D) - married.

gift (No) (Sw) - married.

gigno (L) - to beget; to bear; to be born; to produce.

Gilebertus, Gislebertus (L) - Gilbert.

giorno (It) - day.

giovane, (It) - young.

giovine (It) - young.

giovanetto (It) - boy.

giv. - giving; given.

Glams. (W) - Glamorgan.

Glavorna, Glaworna (L) - Gloucester.

glebe - the cultivable land by a parish church or ecclesiastical benefice; soil.

Glevum (L) - Gloucester.

Glocestria (L) -Gloucester.

gloris (L) - sister-in-law.

glos (L) - sister-in-law.

Gloucs. (E) - Gloucester.

Gloucestresc (L) - Gloucestershire.

Gloveceastria, Glovernia (L) - Gloucester.

gm. - *grandmother.

Godefridus (L) - Godfrey.

Godf. - *Godfather.

Godm. - *Godmother.

gods (D) - landed estate.

goodman - householder; husband; an appellation of civility, equivalent to "Mister" or the like, prefixed to the names of persons, as yeomen, under the rank of gentlemen. (see SYA p. 141).

goodwife - the same as goodman for the female sex.

gor hendaid (W) - 2nd great grandfather.

gorss-tante (G) - grand aunt.

gor wyr (W) - great-grandson.

gor wyres (W) - great-granddaughter.

gosse (Sw) - boy.

Gotebg Bohus. (Sw) - Göteborg & Bohus.

Gotld. (Sw) - Gotland.

gp. - *grandparents.

gr. - grand; great (qq.v.); *grant; *graduate.

G.R. - grave record.

grand____ - standing in the second or some more remote degree of ancestry or descent; two or more generations removed; generally used in composition, as grandfather, grandson, granduncle, grandniece, etc. Abbr. - g; gr.

grandaevus (L) - of great age, old.

grand mère (Fr) - grandmother.

grand oncle (Fr) - granduncle.

grandonkel (D) - granduncle.

grand-onkel (No) - granduncle.

grand père (Fr) - grandfather.

grandtante (D) - grandaunt.

grand tante (Fr) - grandaunt.

grand-tante (No) - grandaunt.

grant - a general term applicable to all transfers of real property.

Granta, Grantanus Pons (L) - Cambridge.

grantee - one to whom a grant is made.

grantor - a person by whom a grant or conveyance is made.

gravestone inscription - the inscription on a stone laid over or erected near a grave. (for information on customs of the past regarding gravestones see SYA pp. 77-78).

gr/d/o - *granddaughter of.

great - older, younger or more remote by one generation - used before grand to indicate one degree more remote in the direct line of descent; as, great grandfather (a grandfather's or grand-

mother's father); Abbr. -
*g.; gr.; gt. Great great
grand father is one more
generation removed and
may also be writen: 2
gg father; second great
grandfather. Mother; un-
cle; aunt, son, daughter,
nephew and niece may all
be used in combinations
as above.

Gregorian Calendar - the
calendar now in general
use, introduced by Pope
Gregory VIII A.D. 1582
and adopted by Great
Britain and the English
colonies in America in
1752; a reformation of
the Julian Calendar. (q.
v., also double-dating;
GGr p. 320 ff; SYA pp.
135-38; 1953 HB p. 220).

Grenteburga (L) - Cam-
bridge.

gr. f. - *grandfather.
gr. m. - *grandmother.
Gron. (Ne) - Groningen.
grootmoeder (Du) - grand-
mother.
grootvader (Du) - grand-
father.
gross-, grösser- (G) -
great, greater.
grossmutter (G) - grand-
mother.
gross-onkel (G) - grand-
uncle.
Gross-tante (G) - Grand
aunt.
grossvater (G) - grand-

father.
gr/s/o - *grandson of.
g.s. - *gravestone
gt. - great (q.v.).
Gt. Br. - Great Britian.
gt. gr - great grand (q.v.).
GTT. - gone to Texas.
gu. - gules (q.v.).
Gualterus (L) - Walter.
guardian - one who has, or
is entitled to, the care and
management of the per-
son or property, or both,
of another, as of a minor
or of a person incapable
of managing his own af-
fairs.
gudmoder (D) - godmother.
Guillelmus (L) - William.
gules (her) - red.
Gull. (Ic) -Gullbringusysla
gutshof (Sz) - farm.
gutt (No) - boy.
gweddw, gwraig weddw (W)
- widow.
gweddw, gwr gweddw (W) -
widower.
gwlad (W) - country.
gwr (W) - husband, man.
gwraig (W) - wife.

H

h. - heir (q.v.); husband.
1/h, 2/h - *first husband,
*second husband, etc.
habeas corpus - a writ requiring the body of a person to brought before a
judge or court. (L) You
shall have the body.
habitator (L) - dweller, in-

habitant.

hac (L) - by or this way or side; here; hither.

Hadlev. (D) - Haderslev.

Hainaut. (Bel)- Henegouwen

half aunt - the half sister of a parent.

half brother - a brother by one parent only.

half cousin - the child of half uncle or half aunt.

half uncle - the half brother of a parent.

hameau (Fr) - hamlet.

hamlet - a small group of houses belonging to a parish or village; a little cluster of houses in the country.

Hamps. (E) - Hampshire.

Hann. (G) - Hannover.

Hantonia (L) - Hampshire.

härad (Sw) - local government area.

Haraldus (L) - Harold.

Harefordia (L) - Hereford.

haudattu (Fi) - buried.

Hawisha (L) - Hawise.

hearsay - something heard from another; rumor; report.

hearsay evidence - out-of-court statements, oral or written, when offered as evidence. Not acceptable as evidence under ordinary circumstances.

heb briodi (W) - unmarried.

Heidelbg. (G) - Heidelberg.

heir - one who inherits, or is entitled to succeed to the possession of, any property after the death of its owner; inheritor. Anciently the heir, coheir, heiress or coheiress had the right to transmit arms to their issue, the details of the manner of which have always been regulated by strict rules. The inheritance of land or money does not enter in when considered under the rules of heraldry (q.v.).

heiress - a female heir. (see heir).

Heisa (L) - In Kent.

Helena (L) - Helen.

helmet (Her) - a defensive covering for the head.

hendad (W) - grandfather.

hen daid (W) - great-grandfather.

hen ewythr (W) - granduncle.

hen fam (W) - grandmother.

hen fodryb (W) - grandaunt.

hen nain (W) - great-grandmother.

Henoforthum (L) - Hereford

Henricus (L) - Henry.

Heortiforda (L) - Hertford.

Her. - Heraldry.

hera (L) - mistress of a house; lady; dame.

herald - in Great Britain and Ireland, an officer charged with the care of genealogies and armorial bearings (qq.v.); one who publishes or announces; a forerunner. (see Heralds' College).

heraldic - of or pertaining to heralds or heraldry (qq.v.).

heraldic bearing - heraldic symbol or emblazonment

heraldry - the art or science of a herald (q.v.); the art practice, or science of recording genealogies and blazoning arms, or ensigns armorial. (see SYA pp. 144 146; GGR pp. 217-222; also heir, Heralds' College).

Heralds' College - in England, a corporation, dependent upon the crown, instituted about 1460-85, consisting of Kings-of-arms, Heralds and pursuivants. This retains from the Middle Ages the charge of the armorial bearings of persons privileged to bear them, as well as of the genealogies and kindred subjects. (see heraldry).

heredis (L) - heir.

hereditary societies - associations formed by descendants to honor common ancestors or groups of ancestors, such as Daughters of the American Revolution, First Families of Virginia, etc.

hereditas (L) - heirship; inheritance.

Hereffordscr' (L) - Herefordshire.

Herefs. (E) - Hereford.

hermana (Sp) - sister.

hermano (Sp) - brother.

herred (D) - divison or district with in a county.

hers. - *herself.

Hertfordia (L) - Hertford.

Herts. (E) - Hertford.

herus (L) - master of the house or family; lord; owner.

Hess./N (G) - Hessen/Nassau.

HG. - High German.

hic (L) - here; in this matter.

hic jocet sepultus (L) - here lies buried. Abbr. - H.J.S.

hic requiescit in pace (L) - here rests in peace. Abbr. - H.R.I.P.

hic sepultus (L) - hic situs (q.v.).

hic situs (L) - here is buried. Abbr. - h.s.

hide of land - a measure of land common in Domesday Book and in old English charters varying from 80 to 120 acres.

Hieremias (L) - Jeremiah.

Hieronymus (L) - Jerome.

hiippakunta (Fi) - bishopric or diocese.

hija (Sp) - daughter.

hija natural (Sp) - natural or illegitimate daughter.

hija politica (Sp) - daughter in-law.

hijo (Sp) - son.

hijo natural (Sp) - illegitimate son.

hijo politico (Sp) - son-in-law.

hinter (D) - posterior.

hist. - history, historian.

historical method or form - the mode or system used by writers and teachers (genealogists) basing their work and teachings upon the facts shown by historical research and the inductions to be drawn from them. (see legal method).

hims. - *himself.

Hjorrg. (D) - Hjørring.

H.J.S. - hic jocet sepultus (q.v.).

H.M. - His or Her Majesty.

h.m. - hoc mense (q.v.).

Hnapp. (Ic) - Hnappadalssysla.

hoc loco (L) - in this place.

hoc mense (L) - in this month. Abbr. - h.m.

hoc tempore (L) - at this time. Abbr. - h.t.

Hohenz. (G) - Hohenzollern.

Holbaek (G) - Holbaek.

Holland Dutch - immigrants from The Netherlands who settled in the U.S. (Not Pennsylvania Dutch q.v.).

holographic (Law) - of wills, totally in the handwriting of the testator (witnesses not required).

hombre (Sp) - man.

homestead application - the application filed under the Homestead Act authorizing the sale of public lands, in parcels of 160 acres to each settler. (see ABC p. 75).

homme (Fr) - man.

homo (L) - man.

hon. - *honor; honorary; honorable (q.v.).

honorable - a title of distinction given to certain officials and others, usually simply as a courtsey title. Abbr. - hon.

hora (L) - hour; season (of the year); time.

Hordald. (No) - Hordaland.

hrepp (Ic) - rural municipality or division of county.

H.R.I.P. - hic requiescit in pace (q.v.).

h.s. - hic situs (q.v.).

h.t. - hoc tempore (q.v.).

Hte⁄Garonne (Fr) - Haute⁄Garonne.

Hte⁄Loire (Fr) - Haute⁄Loire.

Hte⁄Marne (Fr) - Haute⁄Marne.

Hte.⁄Saone (Fr) - Haute⁄Saône.

Htes⁄Alpes (Fr) - Hautes⁄

Alpes.

Hte/ Savoie (Fr) – Haute/ Savoie.

Htes/ Pyr. (Fr) – Hautes/ Pyénées.

Hte/ Vienne (Fr) – Haute/ Vienne.

Ht./Rhin. (Fr) – Haut/Rhin.

Hugo (L) – Hugh.

Huguenot – a French Protestant in the 16th and 17th centuries; one of the members of the Reformed or Calvinistic communion who were driven by the thousands into exile in England, Holland, Germany and America.

hujus (L) – his; this.

hujus mense (L) – this month's.

Humfredus (L) – Humfrey.

hund. – hundred (q.v.).

hundred – in England, later also in Ireland, a division of a county, formerly having its own local court (the hundred court or moot); also, the body of land holders and residents of the hundred; in U.S., derived from the Eng. hundred, formerly existed in Virginia, Maryland, and Pennsylvania and still survives in Delaware. Abbr. – hund.

Huntedon (L) –Huntingdonshire.

Huntindonia, Huntundona(L)

– Huntingdon.

Hunts. (E) – Huntingdon.

husbandman – a master of the household; a farmer. Abbr. – *husbn.

husbandry – farming; the various branches of agriculture.

husbn. – *husbandman (q. v.).

husbonde (D) – husband.

husmand (D) – small farmer owning own house.

hustru (D) (No) (Sw) – wife.

hynaf (W) – eldest.

hynafiad (W) – ancestor.

I

i – sometimes interchanged with j in Old English.

I. – *inventory (q.v.).

iacet hic (L) – here lies. Abbr. – i.h.

iäkäs (Fi) – aged, old.

ib.; ibid. – ibidem (q.v.).

ibidem (L) – in the same place; the same book, chapter, page, etc. Abbr. – ib.; ibid.

idem (L) – the same.

idem quod (L) – the same as. Abbr. – i. q.

id est (L) – that is. Abbr. – i.e.

I.D.N. – In Dei Nomie – in the Name of God.

i.e. – id est (q.v.).

I./et/ L. (Fr) – Indre/et/ Loire.

I./et/V. (Fr) – Ille/et/Vilaine.

ieuaf, ieuengaf (W) - youngest.

i.f. - ipse fecit (q.v.).

ign. - *ignorant; ignotus (q.v.).

ignotus (L) - unknown; low born.

i.h. - iacet hic (q.v.).

ikä (Fi) - age.

ikäinen (Fi) - aged.

il.; i-l. - *in-law (q.v.).

Ill. - Illinois.

ille (L) - he; she; it; that one, the aforesaid; the very same.

illégitime (Fr) - illegitimate.

illegittimo (It) - illegitimate.

im alter von (G) - aged.

immigrant - one who immigrates; one who comes to a country for the purpose of permanent residence; the correlative of emigrant (q.v.).

imprimis (L) - in the first place; chiefly; especially

incl. - included, inclusive.

incognitus (L) - unknown.

incola (L) - an inhabitant.

incompertus (L) - unknown.

Ind. - Indiana; *Indians.

inde (L) - thence; from that place; from that time

indenture - a mutual agreement between two or more parties, whereof each party has usually a counterpart or duplicate;

a contract by which an apprentice is bound to a master; a formal or official document, as a certificate or an inventory (originally one prepared in duplicate).

Ind. T.; Ind. Ter. - Indian Territory.

indidem (L) - from the same place or thing.

ined. - ineditus (q.v.).

ineditus (L) - not made known; unpublished. Abbr. - ined.

inf. - *infant; *informed.

infans (L) - childish; speechless; muted; little child.

infans cui quis in baptismo sponsor exstitit (L) - godchild.

infante (It) - infant.

info. - *information.

infra (L) - under; below.

inh. - *inherited.

inhab. - *inhabitant.

inheritance - the acquisition of property, real or personal by one person as heir to another; that which is or may be inherited.

inheritor - heir; he that inherits. (see inheritance).

inhibition - restraint; prohibition; a writ from a higher court staying an inferior judge from further proceedings in a specific case.

in-law - a relative by marriage. (cousin-in-law, son-in-law, relative-in-law, (qq.v.). Abbr. - *il; *-l.

in loc. cit. - in loco citato (q.v.).

in loco citato (L) - in the place cited. Abbr. - in loc. cit.

in mem. - in memoriam (q. v.).

in memoriam (L) -in memory of. Abbr. - in mem.

innubus (L) - unmarried.

innupta (L) - unmarried.

inq. - *inquiry.

inquilinus (L) - of foreign birth; inmate; lodger.

ins. - *insert.

institus (L) - inborn; natural adopted.

int. - *intentions.

int. - interested.

inter (L) -between; among; in comparison.

intermarriage - reciprocal marriage, as between two families tribes or casts; consanguineous marriage; in breeding.

intestate - dying without having made a will (he died intestate).

intestatus (L) - intestate.

inuptus, inupta (L) - unmarried.

inv. - *inventory (q.v.).

inventory - an account, catalogue, or schedule, made by an executor or administrator, of all the goods and chattels, and sometimes of the real estate, of a deceased person. Abbr. - *I.; *inv.; invt.

Invern. (Sc) - Inverness.

invt. - inventory (q.v.).

I. of Man (E) - Isle of Man.

I. of Wight (E) - Isle of Wight.

ipse fecit (L) - he did it himself. Abbr. - i.f.

ipso facto (L) - by the act itself.

i.q. - idem quod (q.v.).

Ir. - Irish, Ireland.

Ire. - Ireland.

isä (Fi) - father.

Isabella (L) -Isabel, Elizabeth.

isänsetä (Fi) - granduncle.

isäntäti (Fi) - grandaunt.

Isiacum (L) - Oxford.

Isidis Vadum (L) - Oxford.

isoäidinäti (Fi) - great-grandmother.

isoäiti (Fi) - grandmother.

isoisä (Fi) - grandfather.

isoisänisä (Fi) great-grandfather.

isoisänisän isoisänisä (Fi) - 4th great-grandfather.

isoisän isoisä (Fi) - 2nd great-grandfather.

isoisän isoisänisä (Fi) - 3rd great-grandfather.

issue - progeny; a child or children; offspring.

Isuria (L) - Yorkshire.

Isurovicum (L) - York.

It. - Italy or Italian.

iunioris (L) - juvenis (q. v.) (see also "J").

# J

j - sometimes interchanged with "i" in Old English (iij ⩴ 3, Roman Numeral).

jaar (Du) - year.

Jacobus (L) - James, Jacob.

jahr (G) - year.

Jälkisäädös (Fi) - will, testament.

Jamtld. (Sw) - Jämtland.

Johanna (L) - Joan, Jane.

Johannes (L) - John.

jointure - a joint tenancy of an estate, or the estate so held; an estate settled on a wife to be taken by her in lieu of dower.

jongen (Du) - boy.

jongste (Du) - youngest.

Jonkpg. (Sw) - Jönköping.

jour (Fr) - day.

jour. - journal (q.v.).

journal - a diray; an account of daily transactions and events; a record of transactions kept by a deliberate body or assembly. Abbr. - jour.

joven (Sp) - young.

Jr. - junior (q.v.).

juba (L) - crest (of a helmet) (see coat-of-arms).

jud.; *judic. - judicial; *judicious.

juengster, juengst (G) - youngest.

jugo (L) - to marry; to join.

Julian Calendar - the calendar introduced by Julius Ceasar in 46 B.C. and replaced by the Gregorian Calendar (q.v.) 1582 A.D.

jun. - junior (q.v.).

junior (L) - younger. During the Middle Ages and later the terms Jr. and Sr. applied only until the eldest died, then Jr. might change to Sr. if he also had a son with the same name. Thus, he might be Jr. the fore part of his life and Sr. the latter. Abbr. Jr.; jun.; junr.

junr. - junior (q.v.).

juv. - juvenis (q.v.).

juvenalis (L) - youthful.

juvenca (L) - young cow; girl.

juvencus (L) - young bullock; young man.

juvenilis (L) - youthful.

juvenis (L) - young. Abbr. - juv.

# K

k. - *killed; king.

Kanc', Kantia (L) - Kent.

Kans. - Kansas.

kantaisä (Fi) - progenitor.

kanton (Sz) - state. (canton)

Käräjäkunta (Fi) - subdivision of a judicial district.

Karlegion (L) - Chester.

Karlsr. (G) - Karlsruhe.

kastettu (Fi) - baptized.

kauppala (Fi) - smaller city.

kaupunki (Fi) - city.

kerk (Du) - church parish.

Kihlakunta (Fi) - local government area.

Kincard. (Sc) - Kincardine.

kind (Du) (G) - child.

kindred - belonging to the same family or race; related.

king-of-arms - the chief heraldic officer of a country. (see heraldry; Heralds' College).

kirchen-gemeinde (G) - church parish.

kirk (Scot) - church.

Kirkby's Inquest - a survey of the English county of York taken by John de Kirkby 1284-5 A.D. (see GGR p. 229).

Kirkcubd. (Sc) - Kirkcudbright.

kirkjustadur (Ic) - church place.

Kjos. (Ic) - Kjosarsysla.

klein (G) - little.

kleindochter (Du) - granddaughter.

kleinkind (G) - infant.

kleinzoon (Du) - grandson.

kn. - *known.

knabe (G) - boy.

knight - a military attendant, servant, or follower; in feudal times a mounted man-at-arms serving a king or other superior, commonly in return for a tenure of land, especially, one, generally of noble birth, who, after serving regularly as a page and squire was admitted to a special military rank; in modern times, a man upon whom a corresponding dignity has been conferred by a sovereign in recognition of personal merit. Abbr. - knt.

knight bachelor - a knight of the most ancient, but lowest, order of English knights, and not a member of any order of chivalry.

knt. - knight (q.v.).

kommune (D) - a municipality.

kone (D) - wife.

Konstz. (G) - Konstanz.

kontrakt (Sw) - rural deanery containing a number of rectoral districts.

köping (Sw) - commercial center without a city charter.

Koppbg. (Sw) - Kopparberg.

Kreis (G) - county.

Krnstad. (Sw) - Kristianstad

Kronobg. (Sw) - Kronoberg.

kusin (Sw) - cousin.

kusine (D) (No) - female cousin.

kuollut (Fi) - died.

kuollut jättämättä rintaper-
illistä (Fi) - died with-
out issue.

kuukausi (Fi) - month.

kvinde (D) - woman.

kvinna (Sw) - woman.

kvinne (No) - woman.

Ky. - Kentucky.

kylä (Fi) - village.

kyrke byn (No) - sub-division of a parish.

L

l. - liber (q.v.).

L.; *(L) - Latin (q.v.).

La. - Louisiana.

lääni (Fi) - county.

labr. - *laborer.

Laetitia (L) - Lettice.

lamina - a thin plate. The
acetate foil welded to
both sides of a document,
after sterilization to
help preserve it.

laminate - Cover with
laminae (q.v.).

län (Sw) - county.

Lancastra (L) - Lancashire

Lancastria (L) - Lancaster.

Lancs. (E) - Lancashire.

land (D) (Du) (G) (No) (Sw) -
country.

land appilcation - a formal
request for rights in, or
eventual title to public
lands.

Land Entry Papers - docu-
ments filed in connec-
tions with entry on public
land. (see ABC p. 74).

landgemeinde (G) - village,
rural municipality.

land grant - a grant of land
by the government, esp.
for roads or railroads, or
for agricultural or in-
dustrial colleges.

Landinium (L) - London.

land records - various records which have been
made regarding the
transfer of land from
the government to indi-
viduals and from person
to person. (see ABC p.
74; GGR p. 81).

landsby (D) - village.

landskap (Sw) - older name
for län, but with different
bounds.

langen (G) - long.

Lania (L) - Lancashire.

lanius (L) - butcher.

lapseton (Fi) - childless.

lapsi (Fi) - child.

Lat. - Latin (q.v.).

Latin - the language of ancient Latium and of Rome
and until modern times
the dominant language of
school, church and state
in western Europe. Be-
cause of its widespread
use in recording gene-
alogical data, we present
this index with many of
the more common terms
and their translations to
assist you when search-

ing the older records. Abbbr. - L.; *(L); Lat.

Laurentius (L) - Lawrence.

L.C. - Library of Congress ld. - *land.

L.D.S. - Church of Jesus Christ of Latter-Day Saints (Mormon).

leeftijd (Du) - age.

Legacestra (L) - Chester.

Legacestria, Legecestria (L) - Leicester.

legacy - something coming from an ancestor or predecessor; a gift of property by will, esp. money or other personal property.

legal description - the description of a particular parcel of land, according to the official plat of survey.

legal method - documentary method of recording history or genealogy. Each and every step or point is established by original, certified or photostat copies, acceptable in court. (see historical method).

legate - an ambassador or envoy; a delegate or messenger; under Roman History a govenor or assiastant to the govenor of a province.

legatee - one to whom a legacy is bequeathed.

Legio VI Victrix (L) - York.

Legio XX Victrix (L) - Chester.

Legionum Urbs (L) - Chester.

Legoria (L) - Leicester.

Leicestresc' (L) - Leicestershire.

Lecestria, Leogereceastria, Legrecastrum, Licestria, Ligeria, Ligrecastrum, Legoria (L) - Leicester.

Leics. (E) - Leicester.

leskimies (Fi) - widower.

L./et/C. (Fr) - Loir/et/Cher.

L./et/G. (Fr) - Lot/et/Garonne.

letter of attorney - see power of attorney.

letters of administration - the instrument by which an administrator or administratrix is authorized to administer the goods or estate of a deceased person.

letters testamentary - an instrument issued by a court or public official authorizing an executor to take control of and dispose of the estate of a decedent.

letzter wille (G) - last will, testament.

li. - *lived; *living.

lib. - liber (q.v.).

liber (L) - book; free spoken; wine. Abbr. - l.; lib.

liberi (L) - children; grand-children.

liberty (E) - a special division of a parish or town.

lic. - *licence.

Lidocollina (L) - Lincoln.

Lieg. (Bel) - Luik.

liege - a liege lord; a feudal superior to whom allegiance and service are due; a liege subject; a vassal bound to feudal service and allegiance; a liege man.

Lieut. - Lieutenant.

Lincolnia, Lincolinum (L) - Lincoln.

Lincolnscr' (L) - Lincolnshire.

Lincs. (E) - Lincoln.

Lindecolina, Lindecollinum, Lindocollinum (L) - Lincoln.

Lindonium (L) - London.

Lindum, Lindum Colonia (L) - Lincoln.

lineage - ancestry or extraction (See lineal).

lineal - consisting of, or being in, a direct line of ancestry or descendants; descended in a direct line; in the line of succession through lineage. Collateral relationship is not "lineal" though the expression "collateral lines" is not uncommon.

Lippe/ Det. (G) - Lippe/ Detmold.

liv. - *living; *lived.

liv. abt. - *lived about.

l.l. - loco ladato (q.v.).

ll. - lines.

locale - a place or locality.

locality file - the geographical catalogue of a genealogical library.

loc. cit. - loco citato (q.v.).

loco (L) - to place; to lay; to let for hire; to farm out.

loco citato (L) - in the place cited. Abbr. - loc. cit.

loco laudato (L) - in the place cited. Abbr. - l.l.

locus (L) - place; position; rank; place of the seal.

Loer. (G) - Loerrach.

Loire/Inf (Fr) - Loire/Inférieure.

Loncastria (L) - Lancaster.

Lond. (E) - London.

Londinia, Londinium, Londinium Augusta, Londinum, Londonia (L) - London.

longeavus (L) - of great age; ancient.

Longfd. (Ire) - Longford.

loyalist - in the American Rev., one opposed to separation from Great Britain. (see ABC p. 71).

l.s. - locus sigilli (q.v.).

Lucas (L) - Luke.

Lucia (L) - Lucy.

ludimagister (L) - schoolmaster.

Lundinium, Lundonia (L) - London.

Lunia (L) - Lancashire.

Lux. (Bel) - Luxemburg.

## M

M.; m. - man; maritus (q.v.); married.

m/1, m/2 -*married first, *married second, etc.

maa (Fi) - country.

maakunta (Fi) -older name for lääni, but with different bounds.

maand (Du) - month.

maaned (D) - month.

maatila (Fi) - farm.

mab, map (W) -son, son of.

Mabilia, Mabilla (L) - Mabel.

Mac, (prefix) - Scotch Gaelic and Irish signifying son.

madre (It) (Sp) - mother.

maedchen (G) - girl, maiden.

maggiornato (It) - eldest, firstborn.

magna (L) - great.

Magna Charta; Magna Carta - the Great Charter to which the English barons forced King John to affix his seal June 15, 1215; a constitution guaranteeing rights and privileges.

maiden name - the name of a woman prior to marriage.

Maior (L) - Mayor.

Maj. - Major.

major natu (L) - (in date)
prior.

Major - Mayor.

majores (L) - ancestors.

majoris (L) - greater; older.

mak. - *making.

maka (Sw) - wife.

make (Sw) - husband.

Malmhs. (Sw) - Malmöhus.

mam (W) - mother.

man (Du) (Sw) - husband, man.

Man. (Can) - Manitoba.

månad (Sw) - month.

mand (D) - husband, man.

måned (No) - month.

mann (G) - man.

mann (No) - husband, man.

Mannh. (G) - Mannheim.

manor -house against which geld (q.v.) was charged; hence, the land represented in the house, or any plot of land treated as a unit for that purpose; a landed estate or territorial unit, orig. of the nature of a feudal lordship; the mansion of a lord and the land pertaining to it.

manuscript -a composition written with the hand, as an ancient book, document, etc., or an unprinted modern book, piece of music, etc. Abbr. - ms.; MS.; plural Mss.; mss.

map (W) - son of.

Margareta (L) - Margaret.

Margeria (L) - Margery.

mari (Fr) – husband.

Maria (L) – Mary.

marido (Sp) – husband.

marié, mariée (Fr) – married.

marita (L) – married woman; wife.

maritato (It) – married.

marito (It) – husband.

maritus (L) – bridegroom; (of man) married. Abbr. – M.

marriage bond – a financial guarantee that no impediment to the marriage existed. Furnished by the intended bridegroom or by his friends.

marriage by contract or marriage of convenience – a marriage contracted, rather for the advantage arising out of it, such as keeping an estate in a family, acquiring social position, etc.

marriage license – a written authorization granted by a qualified governmental official to a (named) man and woman to marry.

marriage out of unity – a marriage contrary to the Friends (q.v.) order. Also referred to as "marriage by a priest," "outgoing marriage", marriage out of meeting".

Marta (L) – Martha.

marwodd (W) – died.

marwodd yn ddiepil (W) – died without issue.

Mass. – Massachusetts.

mater (L) – mother; matron; maternal love, etc.

materta magna (L) – grandmother's sister (grandaunt).

matertera (L) – mother's sister; aunt.

matertera magna (L) – grandmother's sister (grandaunt).

matrimonium (L) – matrimony. Abbr. – mm.

Mattaeus (L) – Matthew.

maximus natu (L) – eldest; first born.

Mayflower Compact – an agreement, constituting the first written American constitution, signed by 41 of the Pilgrim Fathers in the cabin of the "Mayflower" Nov. 21, 1620, to serve as a form of government, because the Pilgrims possessed no charter. Many ancestral lines run back to and beyond these Pilgrim Fathers (q.v.). (see 1953 HB p. 220. Puritan)

m. bn. – *marriage banns (see banns).

Md. – Maryland.

md. – *married.

MD. – Middle Dutch.

Me. – Maine.

media (L) – middle.

medicus (L) – physician.

# GENEALOGICAL DICTIONARY 187

meisje (Du) - girl.

Melamon (L) - In Devonshire.

Melezo (L) - In Dorsetshire

memorial - anything intended to preserve the memory of a person or event; a record of memoir; a note; an abstract.

mensis (L) - month.

ment. - *mentioned.

merch (W) - daughter.

Mercia (L) - Mercy.

mère (Fr) - mother.

Merions. (W) - Merioneth.

mes (Sp) - month.

mese (It) - month.

Messrs. - plural of mister (q.v.).

M. et L. (Fr) - Maine et Loire.

M. et M. (Fr) - Meurthe et Moselle.

MHG. - Middle High German.

M.I. - monumental inscription.

mi. - miles, mile.

Mich. - Michigan.

Michaelis (L) - Michael.

microfilm - a strip of photographic film, often of standard motion-picture film size, used for making photographic record on reduced scale of printed matter, manuscripts, etc., as for storage or transmission in small space, which is enlarged for reading. Used extensively for copying genealogical records of all kinds.

Middle English - the English language of the period A.D. 1100-1500.

Middlesexa (L) - Middlesex

Middlesexia (L) - Middlesex.

Middx. (E) - Middlesex.

mies (Fi) - man, husband.

m-i-l. - *mother-in-law.

miles (L) - kinght; soldier.

Milidunum (L) - In Devonshire.

milit. - *military.

militi(a)(s) (L) - miles; military service.

min. - minister; minor; minutes.

minima natu (L) - youngest.

minimus natu (L) - youngest

Minn. - Minnesota.

minoris (L) - lesser; younger.

minority - state or period of being under age or a minor.

mis (W) - month.

Miss. - Mississippi.

Mister - in early times, a title of respect given only to those who held important civil office or were of gentle blood. If a man did not act in accordance with the dignity of the title it was taken away from him. (see SYA p. 141). Abbr. - Mr.

Mistress - in the 17th and 18th centuries the title "Mistress" was one of social distinction as a general rule and did not necessarily mean that the woman to whom applied was or had been married. Sometimes it meant widowhood. Abbr. - Mrs. (see SYA p. 141).

mittel (G) - middle.

Mittelfr. (G) - Mittelfranken.

MLG. - Middle Low German.

Mlle. - Mademoiselle.

M. Lothian (Sc) - Midlothian

MM - *Monthly Meeting (q.v.).

mm. - matrimonium (q.v.).

MM. - Messieurs.

Mme. - Madam.

Mo. - Missouri.

mo. - month; *mother.

moder (D) (Sw) - mother.

modryb (W) - aunt.

moeder (Du) - mother.

moglie (It) - wife.

moiety - about a half; part.

mois (Fr) - month.

Monagn. (Ir) - Monaghan.

monat (G) - month.

Monms. (E) (W) - Monmouth

Monmuthsc', Monovaga, Monumethia (L) - Monmouth.

Mons. - Monsignor.

Mont. - Montana.

Montg. (W) - *Montgomery.

Monthly Meeting - the Society of Friends (q.v.) is regulated by periodic meetings known as Meetings for Business. One or more congregations comprise a Monthly Meeting, held once a month; one or more Monthly Meetings form a Quarterly Meeting, held once in three months; the Quarterly Meetings within a stated geographical area form a Yearly Meeting, called a Society of Friends. Many records are preserved of these meetings giving much genealogical information The records kept in Monthly Meetings consist of birth, marriage and death, also minutes or proceedings, discussions, condemnations and disownments. Two sets of meetings were kept, one for male and one for female members. (see marriage out of unity). Abbr. - *MM.

mor (D) (No) - mother.

mor. - *mother.

morbroder (D) - mother's brother (uncle).

morbror (Sw) - mother's brother (uncle).

More og R. (No) - More og Romsdal.

morfar (D) (No) (Sw) - mother's father (grandfather).

morfars far (Sw) - mother's father's father (great-grandfather).

morfars mor (Sw) - mother's father's mother (great-grandmother).

mormor (D) (No) (Sw) - mother's mother (grandmother).

mormors far (Sw) - mother's mother's father (great-grandfather).

mormors mor (Sw) - mother's mother's mother (great-grandmother).

mors (L) - death; corpse.

mors farbror (Sw) - mother's father's brother (granduncle).

mors faster (Sw) - mother's father's sister (grandaunt).

mors morbror (Sw) - mother's mother's brother (granduncle).

mors moster (Sw) - mother's mother's sister (grandaunt).

mort, morte (Fr) - died.

mortality schedules - taken by census enumerators in 1850, 1860, 1870 and 1880 they give information as to all persons dying within the twelve months preceeding the taking of the census. They are filed in Washington, D. C. (see ABC p. 117).

morte sua defungi (L) - to die natural death.

mortis (L) - death; corpse.

morto (It) - died.

morto senza prole (It) - died without issue.

moster (D) (Sw) - mother's sister (aunt).

mother - female parent; in early times "mother" might mean mother-in-law, stepmother, or even one not of blood or marital relationship; a title of endearment. (see SYA p. 140).

mother-in-law - the mother of one's husband or wife; a stepmother (not in standard use at present).

movable feast days - see feast days.

Moyses (L) - Moses.

Mr. - Mister (q.v.).

Mrs. - Mistress (q.v.).

Ms.; ms. - manuscript (q.v)

Mss.; mss. - manuscripts.

mtg. - meeting (see Monthly Meeting).

muchacha (Sp) - girl.

muchacho (Sp) - boy.

mujer (Sp) - woman, wife.

municipalsamhälle (Sw) - municipality, community with some local jurisdictions.

murió (Sp) - died.

Murionio (L) - in Dorsetshire.

murió sin hijos (Sp) - died without children.

murió sin sucesión (Sp) -

died without issue.

mutter (G) - mother.

my/d - *my daughter.

Myr. (Ic) - Myrasysla.

mythology - the collective myths describing the gods of a people, esp., demigods and legendary human beings in stories which involve super-nautural elements; the science which treats of myths.

N

n. - natus; *nephew; nomen; north; northern; *nupta (qq.v.); name.

N.A. - National Archives.

nacido, nacio (Sp) - born.

nactus (L) - born.

nai (W) - nephew.

naimaton (Fi) - unmarried.

nain (W) - grandmother.

nainen (Fi) - woman.

naitu (Fi) - married.

nam - *named.

Namur (Bel) - Namen.

nata (L) - daughter.

nat. - *natus (q.v.).

nato (It) - born.

natural son or daughter - actually begotten by one (opp. to adopted), esp., in wedlock; it also means born out of wedlock or il-legitimate; consanguin-eous; Native-born.

naturel, naturelle (Fr) - illegitmate.

natus (L) - birth; age; son; offspring. Abbr. - n.; *nat.

N.B. (E) - North Britain.

N.B. (Can) -New Brunswick

N.bottn. (Sw) -Norrbotten.

N.C. - North Carolina.

n.d. - no date.

N. Dak. - North Dakota.

N.E. - New England.

ne. - northeast.

né, née (Fr) - born.

necrology - an obituary notice or a list of persons who have died within a certain time.

nee - born (placed after the name of a married woman to introduce her maiden name) (Mrs. Jones, nee Smith).

N.E.H. & G.R., - New England Historic & Genea-logical Register.

Nebr. - Nebraska.

neef (Du) - male cousin.

neefje (Du) - nephew.

neefe (G) - nephew.

nephew - a son of one's brother or sister; a son of one's husband's or wife's brother or sister; (in euphemistic use) an illegitimate son of an ecclesiastic; a grandson; a male descendant of more remote degree. Abbr. - *n.

nephew-in-law - husband of one's niece. Abbr. - *neph-i-l.

neph-i-l - *nephew-in-law
(q.v.).

nepos (L) - grandson;
nephew.

nepotis (L) - grandson;
nephew; descendant.

neptis (L) - graddaughter.

Neth. - Netherlands.

neu (G) - new.

Nev. - Nevada.

neveu (Fr) - nephew.

nevø (D) (No) - nephew.

new style calendar - see
Gregorian calendar; dou-
ble dating.

nfi - no further information.

nfk - nothing further known.

Nfld. - Newfoundland in-
cluding Labrador.

N. H. - New Hampshire.

N. Ire. - Northern Ireland.

nicht (Du) - female cousin.

nichte (G) - niece.

nichtie (Du) - niece.

nickname - a name added to
or substituted for the
proper name of a person,
place, etc. a familiar
form of a proper name,
as Jim for James.

Nicolaus (L) - Nicholas.

Nicole (L) - Lincoln.

niece - the daughter of a
brother or sister.

Niederb. (G)-Niederbayern

niese (No) - niece.

nieta (Sp) - granddaughter.

nieto (Sp) - grandson.

niña (Sp) - small girl.

niña pequeña (Sp) - infant
girl.

niño (Sp) - small boy.

niño pequeño (Sp) - infant
boy.

nipote (f) (It) - niece.

nipote (m) (It) - nephew.

nipotina (It) - grand-
daughter.

nipotino (It) - grandson.

N./Isf. (Ic) - Nordur/Isaf-
jardarsysla.

nith (W) - niece.

N.J. - New Jersey.

N. Mex. - New Mexico.

N./Mul. (Ic) -Nordur/Mula-
sysla.

nm. - *name.

nmed. - *was named.

nms. - *names.

nw. - northwest.

nobilitas (L) - high birth;
renown.

No. Brab. (Ne) - North
Brabant.

N./Oestr. (Aus) - Nieder-
oesterreich.

No. Holl. (Ne) - North Holland.

noin (Fi) - about.

nomen (L) - name; family;
Abbr. - n.

non (L) - not.

Non-Conformist - one who
refuses to conform to an
established church or the
Church of England.

Nor. - Norway, Norwégian.

Nordhumbra, Nordhumbria
(L) - Northumberland.

Nordld. (No) - Nordland.

Nordovolca, Norfolcia (L) -
Norfolk.

Norf. (E) - Norfolk.

Norffolca (L) - Norfolk.

Norfolca (L) - Norfolk.

Northamptonia, Northantuna (L) - Northampton.

Northanimbria (L) - Northumberland.

Northantescr' (L) - Northamptonshire.

Northantonia (L) - Northampton.

Northants. (E) - Northampton.

Northimbria (L) - Northumberland.

Northum. (E) - Northumberland.

Northumbria, Northymbria (L) - Northumberland.

Northumberlanda (L) - Northumberland.

not. - *noted.

nothis (L) - spurious; illegitimate.

nothus (L) - spurious, illegitimate.

Notingehamsc', Nottingamia (L) - Nottingham.

Notts. (E) - Nottingham.

nova nupta (L) - bride.

noverca (L) - stepmother.

novus (L) - new; young; fresh.

novus maritus (L) - bridegroom.

n.p. or d. - no place or date.

nr. - near.

N.S. (Can) - Nova Scotia.

N. S. - New Style (of dating since 1752) (see double dating; Julian calendar).

N./Thing. (Ic) - Nordur Thingeviarsysla.

N./Tronglg. (No) - Nord Trøndelag.

nubo (L) - to marry (a husband).

nuncupative - (of wills, etc) oral rather than written; given before witnesses.

nuorin (Fi) - youngest.

nupital - of or pertaining to marriage or the marriage ceremony.

nupta (L) - (of a woman) married. Abbr. - *n.

nuptiae (L) - marriage.

nuptialis (L) - nupital (q.v.).

nuptus (L) - married.

nurus (L) - daughter-in-law; young woman.

N.W. Terr. (Can) - Northwest Territories.

N.X.N. - *no christian name.

N.Y. - New York.

N.Y.G. & B.R. - New York Genealogical and Biographical Record.

N.Z. - New Zealand.

## O

o. - *oath; optimus (q.v.).

O' - a prefix to ancient Irish family names followed by the genitive case of the name of the ancestor, as O'Neil (nom. Niall). Before surnames of females, O' is replaced in Irish by ni, daughter. It prefixes H before a vowel, as Oh Airt, O'Hart. The apostrophe is due to the mistaken idea that O stands for of.

oäkta (Sw) - illegitimate.

OB - *Order Book.

ob. - obiit; obiter (qq.v.).

ob. caelebs (L) - died unmarried.

ober (G) - upper.

Oberbg. (G) - Oberbayern.

Oberfr. (G) - Oberfranken.

obiit (L) - he or she died. Abbr. - ob.; obt.

obiit sine prole (L) - he or she died without issue. (childless). Abbr. - ob.s.p.

obiit sine prole masculus (L) - he or she died without male issue. Abbr. - *ob.s.p.m.

obiit vita patris (L) - died in the lifetime of his or her father. Abbr. - *ob. v.p.

obiter (L) - incidently. Abbr. - ob.

obituary - pertaining to or recording a death.

ob.s.p - obiit sine prole (q.v.).

ob.s.p.m. - *obiit sine prole masculus (q.v.).

obt. - obiit (q.v.).

ob. unm. - *he or she died unmarried.

ob.v.p. - *obiit vita patris (q.v.).

o.c. - only child; opere citato (q.v.).

Occidua Wallia (L) - Cornwall.

OE.; O.E. - Old English (q.v.).

oed (W) - age, aged.

off; *offi. - official.

Offenbg. (G) - Offenburg.

O. F. S. - Orange Free State (So. Africa).

oft. - *often.

ogift (Sw) - unmarried.

O. Gotld. (Sw) - Östergötland.

O. Ijsel. (Ne) - Overijssel (Overyssel).

Okla. - Oklahoma.

Olaus (L) - Olaf, Olave.

oldebarn (D) - great-grandchild.

oldefader (D) - great-grandfather.

oldefar (No) - great-grandfather.

oldemoder (D) - great-grandmother.

oldemor (No) - great grandmother.

Oldenbg. (G) - Oldenburg.

Old English - the English of periods before 1100; Anglo-Saxon; the form of black letters used by English printers from the 15th to the 18th century. Abbr. - OE.; O.E.

old style calandar - see Julian calendar, double-dating. Abbr. - O.S.; o/s.

omkring (No) (Sw) - about.

omstreeks (Du) - about.

oncle (Fr) - uncle.

onecht (Du) - illegitimate.

ongehuwd (Du) - unmarried.

onkel (D) (G) (No) - uncle.

Ont. - Ontario.

O./Oestr. (Aus) - Ober-oesterreich.

oom (Du) - uncle.

o.p. - out of print.

op. cit. - opere citato (q.v.).

operarius (L) - laborer.

opere citato (L) - in the work cited. Abbr. - o.c.; op. cit.

Opfalz. (G) - Oberpfalz.

oppeto (L) - to go to meet; to perish; to die.

oppidanus (L) - of or in a town (other than Rome).

optimas (L) - aristocrat.

optimus (L) - the best. Abbr.- o.

or. (Her) - yellow or gold color.

orbitas (L) - orphanage; widowhood.

orbo (L) - to bereave (of parents, children, etc.).

orbus (L) - bereaved, child-less; parentless.

ord. - ordained; ordinance.

Oreg. - Oregon.

org. - organization.

orig. - origin; original.

origo (L) - beginning; birth; origin.

oriundus (L) - descended; sprung from.

Orkney. (Sc) - Orkney Islands.

orphan - a child bereaved by the death of both parents, or, less commonly, of one parent.

orphan chamber - the chamber or court having jurisdiction over minors, wills, etc., and presided over by the orphan master.

orpan's court - in the U.S. and other countries orphans have been recognized as wards of the state and governmental provision is made for their care through the orphan's courts. The duty of the state to provide for orphans was first recognized in the early part of the 17th century.

ort (G) - place.

ortus (L) - rising; sunrise; birth.

O.S.; o/s - old style calendar (see double-dating; Julian calendar).

Osrfd. (No) - Østfold.

o.t.p. - of this parrish.

oud-oom (Du) - eldest.

oudste (Du) - eldest.

oud-tante (Du) - grandaunt.

overgrootmoeder (Du) - great-grandmother.

overgrootvader (Du) - great-grandfather.

oxgang - a bovate (q.v.).

Oxon. (E) (G) - Oxford.

Oxonia, Oxonium, Oxenforda, Oxfordia, Oxonium (L) - Oxford.

P

p. - page; pater; per; populus; post; pro (qq.v.). *parents, *parentage.

Pa. - Pennsylvania.

p.a. - pro anno; per annum (qq.v.).

padre (It) (Sp) - father.

paese (It) - country.

page - one side of the leaf of a book, etc.; a boy servant or attendant; a youth in training for knighthood. Abbr.;p.; pp. - pages.

país (Sp) - country.

päivä (Fi) - day.

palaeography - old or ancient writing; the science that treats of the writing of the ancients.

palatinate - a province or territory of the palatine or county palatine; a native or inhabitant of the Palatinate.

Palatinate - a state of the old German Empire, lying along the Rhine. The present Palatinate is a district of Bavaria.

palatine - of or pertaining to a palace; possessing royal privileges, as, a count or earl palatine; an officer of an imperial palace; a native or inhabitant of the Palatinate;

a palatinate or county palatine.

Palatines of Pa. - early settlers, who through persecution were driven from their homes along the Rhine River, their home being called the Palatinate (q.v.).

palimpsest - a kind or portion of writing material, as parchment or paper, so prepared that the writing could be erased.

panoply - a full suit of armor; anything defending or protecting completely by covering or enveloping.

pam.; pamph. - pamphlet.

Papist - a Roman Catholic regarded as a partisan of the Pope.

Par. - Parish.

parens (L) - father; mother; parents.

parentis (L) - father; mother; parents.

parento (L) - to offer solemn sacrifice in honor of deceased parents or relatives; to revenge (a person's death by that of another).

parish - originally, in Great Britain and some British colonies, the ecclesiastical unit of area consisting of the circuit or district committed to the charge of one parson

or vicar or other minis-
ter. Originally this dis-
trict consisted of one or
more vills or towns (in
the south of England usu-
ally one, in the north
several). Several par-
ishes make up a Rural
Deanery (q.v.).

parish register - a book
kept for the recording of
all the christenings,
marriages, and burials in
a parish. (see SYA p. 95;
GGR p. 196; 4th Ed. HB
p. 200). Abbr. - *P.R.

parocchia (It) - parish.

paroch - a clergymen in
charge of a parish.

parochia (L) - parish.

parochie (Du) (G) (Ne) -
parish.

parochial - of or pertaining
to a parish.

paroisse (Fr) - parish.

parroquia (Sp) - parish.

parva (L) - little.

passenger list - a ship's
list of passengers. Gen-
erally referring to the
lists of passengers ar-
riving in the U.S. from
European countries. (see
ABC p. 87).

passim (L) here and there,
up and down, far and wide
in a disorderly manner,
confusedly.

pastor (L) - herdsman;
shepherd.

pastorate (Sw) - recortal

district containing more
than one parish.

pat. - patent, patented.

patent - an instrument of
deed making a convey-
ance or grant of public
lands; the land of ter-
ritory so conveyed.

patentee - one to whom a
grant is made, or a pri-
vilege secured, by patent.

pater (L) - father; sire.
Abbr. - p.

pater familias (L) – head of
a household; father of a
family.

paternal - of or pertaining
to a father.

patres (L) - fathers. Abbr.
- pp.

patria (L) - fatherland; native country.

Patricius (L) - Patrick.

patrius (L) - fatherly; paternal; hereditary; in-
nate.

patronymic - in strict
usage, a name formed by
the addition of a prefix or
suffix indicating sonship
or other relationship to
the name of one's father
or paternal ancestor, as
Johnson, son of John –
Macdonald, son of Donald
- Ivanovich, son of Ivan,
etc.

patruelis (L) - cousin on the
father's side.

patruus (L) - (paternal)
uncle; severe reprover.

patruus major (L) -grandfather's brother (granduncle).

pauper (L) - poor man.

pays (Fr) - county or state.

P.C.C. - *Prerogative Court of Canterbury. (see prerogative court); privy council cases (q.v.).

Pc/de/C. (Fr) - Pas/de/Calais.

pchd. - *purchased.

P. C. Y. - *Prerogative Court of York, (see Prerogative court).

peculiar parish - a parish which has been given the authority to administer its business without reference to the control of higher ecclesiastical authorities, such as deans, archdeacons and bishops. In some cases they had the right to probate a will

peculium (L) - a small private property; private property of a son, daughter or slave, held with the father's or master's consent.

P./de/D. (Fr) - Puy/de/Dome

pedigree -an ancestral line or line of descent; a genealogical table.

pédigrée (Fr) - pedigree.

pedwerydd hen daid (W) - 4th great-grandfather.

P. E. I. - Prince Edward Island.

pellex (L) - concubine (of a married man).

Pembs. (W) - Pembroke.

Pennsylvania Dutch - descendants of 18th century settlers in Pa. from SW Germany; their dialect. (not Holland Dutch).

pension lists or records - the lists of pensioners who served in the wars of the U.S. from Revolutionary times on down. The Archivist of the United States, National Archives Washington, D. C. has charge of pension applications (see SYA p. 119; ABC p. 85).

pentre (W) - village.

peo. - *people.

per (L) - by (means of); great; very; through; all over, etc. Abbr. - p.

per annum (L) - by the year; annually. Abbr. - p.a.

pere (Fr) - father.

peregrinus (L) - strange; stranger; foreigner.

perh. - perhaps.

personal property - estate or property that is not real, consisting in general, but not always, of things temporary or movable; chattels.

petite fille (Fr) - granddaughter.

petit fils (Fr) - grandson.

petition - a formally drawn-up request addressed to a person or a body of persons in authority or power, soliciting some favor, right, mercy, or other benefit. Abbr. - *petn.; *petitn.

petitioner - he who petitions Abbr. - *petr.

petitn. - *petition (q.v.).

petn. - *petition (q.v.).

petr. - *petitioner (q.v.).

Petronilla (L) - Parnel, Pernell.

Petrus (L) - Peter.

pfarramt (G) (Sz) - parish (the bounds of Catholic and Protestant parishes are different).

photostat copy - photographic copies; copies of records, maps, etc., made with a photostat, one of the simpler methods of photographing any printed or handwritten material.

P.I. - The Republic of the Philippines.

pieni kaupunki (Fi) - small town.

pieni lansi (Fi) - infant.

pige (D) - girl.

pike (No) - girl.

Pilgrim Fathers - the English separatists who founded the colony of Plymouth, Mass., in 1620. (see Mayflower Compact)

pipe rolls - Eng. Hist., the great or annual, rolls containing the pipes or statements of the account

of the king's revenue, expenses, etc., 1131 to 1833.

piscator (L) - fisherman.

pitäjä (Fi) - civil parish.

plaats (Ne) - place.

plantation - a place planted; an estate, usually large, and cultivated; in Maine, a minor civil division, having a very simple form of government; in Mass., land without trees of merchantable value.

plebes; plebs (L) - common people; populace.

plentyn (W) - infant, child.

plwyf (W) - parish.

poika (Fi) - boy, son.

pojanpoika (Fi) - grandson.

pojanpojanpoika, pojantyttarenpoika (Fi) - greatgrandson.

pojanpojantytär, pojantyttärentytar (Fi) - greatgranddaughter.

pojantytar (Fi) - granddaughter.

pojke (Sw) - boy.

Pomm. (G) - Pommern.

poor law - a law providing for or regulating support of the poor. Started in England 1601, in the U.S. at various times. (see GGR p. 227).

poor law union - see union.

popula (L) - people.

populus (L) - people. Abbr. - p.

post (L) - after. Abbr. - p.

Postal Guide - see U.S. Postal Guide.

posterity - descendants; offspring to the furthest generation.

postridie (L) - on the day after; the next day.

Potboiler - A book, painting etc., executed soley, and often hastily, as a means of subsistence.

potwalloper - literally, pot-boiler; specif., Eng. Hist., one of a certain class of voters (see pot-walloper).

potwalloper - in certain boroughs of England before the Reform Act of 1832 a voter whose qualification for suffrage was the bolling (walloping) of his own pot, that is, the fact of being householder, as proved by his having a separate fireplace where food was cooked for himself and family.

power of attorney - an instrument authorizing one to act as the attorney or agent of the person granting it either generally, or, more often, for some specified limited purpose. Abbr. - p.p.a. (per power of attorney).

PP. - patres (q.v.).

pp. - pages (see page).

p.p.a. - per power of attorney (see power of attorney).

P. R. - Commonwealth of Puerto Rico.

P. R. - *parish register (q.v.).

praedium (L) - land; estate.

praenomen (L) - first name.

prec.; *precd. - preceding.

predecessore (It) - ancestor.

predicator - preacher; esp., a preaching friar.

pre-emption - act or right of purchasing before others; a piece of land occupied under a preemption right. (q.v.).

Pre-Emption Application - an application by a person who had already settled on unappropriated land.

pre-emption right - right given by the Federal public land laws (repealed 1891) to citizens of buyin a quarter section of land or less. (see preemption).

prerogative court - formerly, the court of either of the archbishops (of Canterbury or York in Eng., or Armagh in Ireland), which had jurisdiciton in all cases of wills or administrations, transferred to Court of Probate 1857; the probate court of New Jersey.

preussisch (G) - Prussian.

pridem (L) - long since.

pridie (L) - on the day before.

prima (Sp) - female cousin.

primo (Sp) - male cousin.

primogénito (It) Sp) - eldest, firstborn.

primos hermanos (Sp) - first cousins.

primos segundos (Sp) - second cousins.

priod, prioddodd (W) - married.

priores (L) - ancestors.

Private Land Claim - a claim to land granted to individulas from foreign countries prior to the cession of that land to the U.S. These were in Ala., Ark., Calif., Fla., Ill., Ind., Iowa, La., Mich., Miss., Mo., Colo and N. Mex.

privigna (L) - stepdaughter.

privignus (L) - stepson.

privy council - a secret council; a private, or personal council.

pro (L) - for. Abbr. - p.

pro. - *probate; *proved.

Pro. *Province.

P. R. O. - *Public Record Office.

pro anno (L) - for the year. Abbr. - p.a.

proavia (L) - great-grandmother.

proavus (L) - great grandfather; ancestor.

prob. - probably.

probate - proof; official proof; esp., the proof before a tribunal that an instrument offered is the last will and testament of a person deceased. (see probate court).

probate court - a court for the probate of wills, administration of estates and related matters (see probate).

professional genealogist - one engaged in genealogical research as a vocation; one receiving remuneration for genealogical work. (see amateur genealogist).

progenies (L) - race; family; progeny.

progenitor - an ancestor; a forefather.

progenitores (Sp) - progenitors, ancestors.

proles (L) - offspring; progeny; descendants.

pronepos (L) - great grandson.

proneptis (L) - greatgranddaughter.

pronipota (f) (It) - greatgranddaughter.

pronipote(m) (It) - greatgrandson.

pronurus (L) - wife of a grandson.

proof - an establishment of a fact by evidence.

proofread - to read and mark corrections in; to read in order to detect and mark errors.

prop. - property.

propositus - one whose relations are sought to be ascertained by a genealogical table; intestate.

propr. - proprietor(s).

prosapia (L) -family; pedigree; race.

proved will - a will established as genuine by probate court.

Province - an ecclesiastical jurisdiction comprising a number of dioceses or bishoprics as they are sometimes called, coming under the jurisdiction of an archbishop. There are three in England -Canterbury, York and Wales.

province - an administrative unit of a country; a region of country; a district.

provincia (It) (L) - county, province.

provincie (Du) (Ne) - province, district.

Provinz (G) - province.

provis. - *provision.

provost - a person appointed to superintend, or preside over, something; a person appointed as an official head.

proximo (L) - next month.

Prudentia (L) - Prudence.

ptf. - *plaintiff.

pub. - public; published;

publisher.

public domain - public lands.

pueblo (Sp) - small town.

puella (L) - girl; sweetheart.

puer (L) - child; boy; young man.

pupillus (L) - orphan boy.

Puritan - one of a class of Protestants who arose in the 16th century within the church of England. Because of religious persecution many left their homes forming a large segment of the early population of New England. (see Mayflower Compact; Pilgrim Fathers).

pursuivant - a heraldic officer ranking below a herald; an official attendant of the heralds.

putative - commonly regarded as such; supposed as a putative father.

putilla (L) - little girl.

putillus (L) - little boy.

pymt. - payment.

Pyr./Orient. (Fr) - Pyrenees/Orientales.

Q

q.e. - quod est (q.v.).

qq. v. - quae vide (q.v.).

quadrimus (L) - of four years, four years old.

quae spondet infantis loco (L) - godmother.

quae vide (L) - which see (plural). Abbr. - qq.v.

Quaker - see Friends.

Que. - Quebec.

que (L) - and (used only as an enclitic particle).

quod (L) - that, in that, because; wherefore; although.

quod est (L) - which is. Abbr. - q.e.

quod vide (L) - which see (singular). Abbr. - q.v.

q.v. - quod vide (q.v.).

qy. - query.

R

R.; r. - rector; regins; rex. (qq.v.).

Radnors. (W) - Radnor.

Radulfus (L) - Ralph.

Raga, Ragae, Rhage, Rage (L) - Leicester.

ragazza (It) - girl.

ragazzo (It) - boy.

Rang. (Ic) - Rangarvalla-sysla.

rat. - *rated.

R.C. - Roman Catholic.

re. - *regarding.

reading machine - the machine used for reading microfilms (q.v.). It makes an enlarged image on ground glass. (ABC p. 33).

real estate or property - land and whatever by nature or artificial annexation is part of it or is the means of its enjoyment, as minerals, trees buildings, fences, etc.

rec. - record; recorder.

rector - a clergyman; the ruler or governor of a country; the chief. Abbr. - R.; r.

Redemptioner - one who, wishing to emigrate from Europe to America secured passage on credit, binding himself to be sold into service by the master or owner of the ship for a stipulated time.

Reg. Gen. - Registrar General (q.v.).

regina (L) - queen. Abbr. - R.; r.

register - a book in which entries of acts, occurrences, names, or the like are recorded; a book or system of public records.

Registrar General - the head of any general register office; spec., Eng., the chief official of the General Register Office, Somerset House, London, W.C.2, England.

regius (L) - kingly, royal, regal.

rel. - relative; religion; released.

relationship - connection or alliance by blood or marriage; kinship.

relative-in-law - one who

is related by marriage.
Abbr. - *rel-i-l.

relic - widow, usually followed by "of"; remains.

relict (L) - survivor; widow.

relicta (L) - widow.

relictus (L) - widower.

rel-i-l. - *relative-in-law (q.v.).

rep. - report; representative.

repository - a place, room, etc., where things are deposited or stored; such as: a museum, an archive a burial vault, etc.

repud. - *repudiate.

requiescat in pace (L) - may he or she rest in peace. Abbr. - R.I.P.

res. - research; residence; resides.

Rev. - *Revolutionary War. (q.v.).

rev. - revised.

Revolutionary War - the war of the American revolution, 1775-83. *Rev.; Rev. War.

Rev. War. - Revolutionary War (q.v.).

rex (L) - king; tyrant; master; leader; tutor. Abbr. - R.; r.

Rhinel. (G) - Rheinland or Rheinprovinz.

R.I. - Rhode Island.

Ricardus (L) - Richard.

riding - an administrative district, orig., York,

Eng., but also found in other British colonies and at one time in Pennsylvania and Long Island; divison of the county in Yorkshire comprising a number of wapentakes; from the Saxon triding, i.e., third part. There are the East, North and West Ridings in Yorkshire.

Ringkby (D) - Ringkøbing.

R.I.P. - requiescat in pace (q.v.).

rlnq. - *relinquished.

Robertus (L) - Robert.

Roesia, Rosa, Rosia (L) - Rose.

Rogald. (No) - Rogaland.

Rogerus (L) - Roger.

Roman Numerals - numerals in the Roman system of notation with values as follows:

I or i - one (see J.).
II or ii - two
III or iii - three
IV or iv - four
V or v - five
VI or vi - six
VII or vii - seven
VIII or viii - eight
IX or ix - nine
X or x - ten
L - fifty
C - one hundred
D - five hundred
M - one thousand

The Roman numeral I, when it stands alone, is

number one; when it is placed before another numeral it subtracts one; when it is placed after another numeral it adds one. It is the same with other numerals, if they are placed in front of a numeral of greater value their value is subtracted, if after, their value is added.

Suppose you should write 1953 in Roman numerals. Always the largest number is written first (unless you want to subtract), and the smaller numbers in sequence. In this case the largest number is 1000 which is M. the next largest is 900 which is CM. The third largest number is 50, which is L. The last number is 3 which is III. Hence, 1953 is written MCMLIII.

Suppose you see the letters MDCLXXXV you would say; M - 1000, D - 500, C- 100 (DC-600), L - 50, XXX - 30, (LXXX- 80), and V - 5. Thus, MDCLXXXV - 1685.

Suppose the letters you write down are MDCCC XXXIX. M - 1000, D - 500, CCC - 300, XXX - 30, IX - 9, total 1839.

At one time the letter "K" was used for 250 and "G" for 400.

Romish Priest - a priest of Rome.

Roscom. (Ire) - Rose-common.

Ross & Crom. (Sc) - Ross & Cromarty.

Rotelandia (L) - Rutland.

rovastikunta (Fi) - rural deanery.

Roxb. (Sc) - Roxburgh.

Rural Deanery - see deanery.

ruricola (L) -husbandman.

rus (L) - country; country-seat; farm.

rustica (L) - country girl.

rusticus (L) - rural.

Rutlanda(ia) (L) - Rutland-shire.

Rutlds. (E) - Rutland.

RW - *Revolutionary War.

S

s. - sepultus; son; *spin-ster(qq.v.); *sons; *successor.

s.a. (L) - secundum artem; sine anno (without year).

sa. (Her) - sable; black.

sadt (G) - town, city.

Salopesbiria, Salopia (L) - Shrewsbury, In Shropshire.

Salopescira (L) - Shropshire.

Salzbg. (Aus) - Salzburg.

s and coh - *son and coheir

s and h - *son and heir.

S.A.R. - Sons of the American Revolution.

Sask. - Saskatchewan.

Saxe. (G) - Sachsen or Saxe.

S.C. - South Carolina.

Scand. - Scandinavian.

scatt. - *scattering or *scatered.

Sch./Lippe (G) - Schaumburg/Lippe.

Schles./Holst. (G) - Schleswig/Holstein.

Schwarzw. (G) - Schwarzwald.

schwester (G) - sister.

Scot. - Scotland.

Scotus (L) - Scotchman.

script - handwriting; the characters used in handwriting; a writing.

S.C.V. - Sons of Confederate Veterans.

S. Dak. - South Dakota

sec. - second; secretary; section; sector.

sec. - security

seisen - possession of either land or chattel. Also seizen.

seized of - legally possessed of.

Selk. (Sc) - Selkirk.

Sen. - senior (q.v.).

senecta; senectus (L) - old age.

senex (L) - old man; old woman; aged.

senior - older or elder. Abbr. - Sen.; Sr. (see junior for instability of use).

senium (L) - old age.

señorita (Sp) - young unmarried lady.

senza marito, smaritato (It) unmarried.

sep. - sepultus (q.v.)

Separatist - One who withdraws from a church; a seceder from an established church; a dissenter; nonconformist.

seppolto (It) - buried.

sepulcrum (L) - grave.

sepulta (L) - buried.

sepultado (Sp) - buried.

sepultus (L) - buried. Abbr. - s.; sep.

seqq. - sequentia (q.v.).

sequentia (L) - the following. Abbr. - seqq.

ser. - *servant; *service.

serg. - sergeant.

serkku (Fi) - cousin.

serv.; servt. - servant.

serva (L) - maid servant.

servula (L) - servant girl.

servulus (L) - servant lad.

servus (L) -servant; slave.

setä (Fi) - uncle.

S./ et L. (Fr) - Saone/et/ Loire.

S./ et M. (Fr) - Seine/et/ Marne.

S./et/O. (Fr) - Seine/et/ Oise.

settl. - *settled; *settler.

seurakunta (Fi) - church parish.

sev. - *several.

Sevenbg. (D) - Svendborg.

S. ⁄ Fjord. (No) - Sogn og Fjordane.

sh. - *share; *ship.

shield - the escutcheon or field on which are placed the bearings in coats of arms (q.v.).

shire - a county; one of the counties of Great Britain.

Shrops. (E) - Shropshire.

Sibella (L) - Sybil.

sic (L) - thus; to introduce something that follows (often used parenthetically to show that something has been copied exactly from the original).

Sidneus (L) - Sidney.

signator (L) - signer; witness (to a will).

signatura (L) - signature.

Siluanus (L) - Silas.

sin. - sine (q.v.).

sine (L) - without. Abbr. - Sn.; sin.

sine anno (L) - without year. Abbr. - s.a.

sine loco (L) - without place. Abbr. - s.l.

sine loco, anno, vel nomine (L) - without place, year or name. Abbr. - s.l.a.n.

sine prole (L) - without issue; without children. Abbr. - s.p.

sine prole supersite (L) - without surviving issue (children). Abbr. - s.p.s.

sir (W) - county.

Sir - the distinctive title of a knight or baronet; a title of respect for some notable personage of ancient times.

sir, swydd (W) - shire, county.

*sis.; sist. - sister (q.v.).

sisar (Fi) - sister.

sisarenpoika (Fi) - sister's son (nephew).

sisarukset (Fi) - brothers and sisters.

sis.il.; sis-i-l - *sister-in-law (q.v.).

sister - the daughter of the same parents; a female friend; a female member of a religious community (nun); a nurse in charge of a hospital room. Abbr. - *sis; sist.

sister-in-law - one's husband's or wife's sister; one's brother's wife. Abbr. - *sis.il.; *sis-i-l; *sister-i-l.

Skag. (Ic) - Skagafjardarsysla.

Skanbg. (D) - Skanderborg.

Skarabg. (Sw) - Skaraborg.

skeppslag (Sw) - coastal government area.

s.l. - sine loco (q.v.).

slaegteregister (D) - pedigree.

s.l.a.n. - sine loco, anno, vel nomine (q.v.).

s.l.p. (L) - sine legitima prole; without legitimate issue.

S. ⁄ Manld. (Sw) - Södermanland.

S./Marit. (Fr)- Seine/Maritime.

S./Mul. (Ic) - Sudur/Mulasysla.

Sn. - sine (q.v.).

Snaef. (Ic) - Snaefellsnessysla.

s/o - *son of.

sobrina; sobrinus (L) - first cousin; cousin german; (Sp) niece.

sobrino (Sp) - nephew.

socer; socerus (L) -father-in-law.

soceri (L) -parents-in-law

Society of Friends - see Friends.

söcken (Sw) - civil or political parish.

socrus (L) -mother-in-law.

soeur (Fr) - sister.

sogn (No) - parish.

sogne (D) - parish.

sohn (G) - son.

So. Holl. (Ne) -Zuid Holland (South Holland).

Sokn (Ic) - parish.

sol. - *soldier.

soltero (Sp) - unmarried.

Som. (E) - Somerset.

Somersata, Somerseta, Somersetania, Somersetensis, Somertunensis Comitatus, Sumersetanea, Sumertunensis, Summurtunensis Paga (L) - Somersetshire.

Somerset House - where the registers of births, marriages, and deaths of England and Wales (1837 to present) are kept. Somerset House, London, W.C.2, England.

son - male child or person in relation to his parents; one adopted as a son; a familiar term of address. (see SYA p. 139)

son (Sw) - son.

Søn (D) - son.

sondotter(Sw)-son's daughter (granddaughter).

son.il.; son-i-l - *son-in-law.

son-in-law - the husband of one's daughter; a stepson

sønn (No) - son.

sønnedatter (D) - son's daughter (granddaughter).

sønne-datter (No) - son's daughter (granddaughter)

sønnesøn (D) - son's son (grandson).

sønne-sønn (No) - son's son (grandson).

sønnesønsdatter (D) - son's son's daughter (great-grand-daughter).

sønnesønssøn (D) - son's son's son (great-grand-son).

sonson (Sw) - son's son (grandson).

sonsons dotter (Sw) - son's son's daughter (great-granddaughter).

sonsons son (Sw) - son's son's son (great-grand-son).

sorella (It) - sister.

soror (L) - sister; female

companion or friend.
Abbr. - Sr.

sororis (L) - sister.

sororis filia - see filia
sororis.

søster (No) (D) - sister.

søsterdatter (D) - sister's
daughter (niece).

søstersøn (D) - sister's son
(nephew).

sou. - *south, southern.

source references - references to books, mss.,
registers, publications,
etc., wherein is found the
information on which the
author has based his
premise or writings. (see
GGR p. 221).

Southeria (L) - Surrey.

Southsexena (L) - The
County of Sussex.

s.p., (L) - sine prole; without issue. (q.v.).

spädbarn (Sw) - infant.

spädebarn (D) - infant.

spebarn (No) - infant.

spell. - *spelling; *spelled.

spinster - a woman still
unmarried; one who
spins. Abbr. - *S. *spr.

sponsor (L) - bondsman;
surety. Abbr. - *spr.; *S.

sponsus (L) - betrothed;
bridegroom; suitor.

sposa (It) - wife.

sposo (It) - husband.

spr. - *spinster; *sponsor
(qq.v.).

s.p.s. - sine prole supersite (q.v.).

spurius (L) - illegitimate
child or birth.

Sr. - senior; soror (qq.v.).

Sr. (before a Name) - Sir.

srnms - *surnames.

S.S. - supra scriptum (q.v.).

SS. - Santi (It) - Saints.

Sta. -Santa (It) -Saint, fem

staat (G) - state.

stad (D) (Du) (Ne) (No) (Sw)
- city.

stadt (G) (Sz) - city, town.

stadtgemeinde (G) - urban
municipality.

Staffordia, Staffordsc' (L) -
Staffordshire.

Staffs (E) - Stafford.

stamfader (D) (Sw) - an-
cestor.

stamfar (No) - progenitor,
ancestor.

stamtavia (Sw) - pedigree.

stamtavle (No) -genealogi-
cal table.

stamtre (No) - pedigree,
genealogical tree.

standesamt (G) - civil registrar's office.

starb (G) - died.

starb kinderlos (G) - died
without issue.

State of Franklin - see
Franklin, State of.

Status Plat - a copy of the
plat or survey upon which
has been diagrammed and
noted such information as
is necessary to deter-
mine the Federal owner-
ship of public lands and
resources.

Steafordensis (L) -Of Stafford.

Steierm.(Aus) -Steiermark

stemma, stemma gentile (L) - pedigree.

Steofordensis (L) -Of Stafford.

step - a prefix indicating connection between members of a family by the remarriage of a parent, and not by blood. (see SYA p. 140).

stepchild - a child of one's husband or wife by a former marriage. (see step)

stepfather - the husband by remarriage of one's mother.

Stephanus (L) - Stephen.

S./Thing. (Ic) - Sudur/Thingeyjarsysla.

stift or biskopsstift (Sw) - bishopric or diocese containing a number of rural deaneries.

still born - dead when born.

stirps - stock; race, family, or branch of family. In law - the person from whom a family or branch of a family is descended. Pl. stirpes.

Stockhm. (Sw) - Stockholm.

Strand. (Ic) - Strandasysla.

S./Tronlg. (No) - Sør Trøndelag.

subnuba (L) - second wife; intruder; rival.

Sudovolca, Suffolcia, Suffolicia (L) - Suffolk.

Sudria (L) - Surrey.

Sudsexa (L) - Sussex.

Suff. (E) - Suffolk.

Suffolca (L) - Suffolk.

sukupuu (Fi) - pedigree.

sukutaulu (Fi) - pedigree.

Sumersetanea, Sumertunensis, Summurtunensis Paga (L) - Somersetshire.

supra scriptum (L) - written above. Abbr. - S.S.

surg. - surgeon.

surname - the name which a person has in common with the other members of his family, as distinguished from his Christian or given name; a family name.

surname file or catalogue - the card index of a genealogical library listing surnames (q.v.).

Surr. (E) - Surrey.

Surra, Surria, Surreia (L) - Surrey.

susceptor (L) -undertaker; receiver; godfather.

Suss. (E) - Sussex.

Sussexia (L) - Sussex.

Suth. (Sc) - Sutherland.

Suthamtunensis Provincia (L) - Hampshire.

Suthregia, Suthreia (L) - Surrey.

Suthriona (L) - Surrey.

Suthsaxonia (L) - Sussex.

Suthsexia (L) - Sussex.

suus (L) - his own, her own its own, their own.

S.U.V. - Sons of Union Veterans.

S.V. - Sons of Veterans.

sw. - *swear; *swore.

Sw. - Sweden, Swedish.

swydd (W) - county.

symbols used by genealogists in Continental Europe appear on many pedigrees and family records. Some, if not all those listed below, might well be used by American genealogists. The following have been checked from several sources and are the most common - you may find many others.

born - * or X

born illegitimate - (*)

christened - ⁓ or =

betrothed - o

married - oo or ∞

divorced - o/o

common law marriage o-o

died - + or † or ⌿

died of battle wounds - + ✕

died in battle ⭢✕ or ✕✕

burial ▢ or ⬚ or ▢

no further issue - ††or ⊕

cremation - ▽

syntynty (Fi) - born.

syskon (Sw) - brothers and sisters.

sysla (Ic) - county.

syster (Sw) - sister.

systerdotter (Sw) - sister's dauther (niece).

systerson (Sw) - sister's son (nephew).

## T

t. - tempore; tomus (qq. v.).

tabularium (L) - archives; register-office.

tad (W) - father.

tag (G) - day.

taid (W) - grandfather.

tak. - *taken.

tante (D) (Du) (Fr) (G) (No) - aunt.

tartan - woolen cloth, checkered or cross barred with narrow bands of various colors, much worn in the Scottish Highlands, where each clan had its distinctive tartan.

tatarabuela (Sp) - 2nd great-grandmother.

tatarabuelo (Sp) - 2nd great-grandfather.

täti (Fi) - aunt.

tectum (L) - house; abode; dwelling.

Telemk. (No) - Telemark.

temp. - tempore (q.v.).

tempore (L) - in the time of. Abbr. - t.; temp.

tempus (L) - time; season; occasion.

ten, tenne (Her) - a stain.

Tenn. - Tennessee.

Terr. Belf. (Fr) - Territoire de Belfort.

test. - testament (q.v.).

testament (Du) (E) (Fr) (G) a formal declaration, usually in writing, of a person's wishes as to the disposition of his property after his death; formerly, a disposition to take effect upon death and relating to personal property (as distinguished from real property), but now will and testament are synonymous. (see will; nuncupative).

testamenta (D) - will, testament.

testamente (No) (Sw) - will, testament.

testamento (It) (Sp) - will, testament.

testamentti (Fi) - will, testament.

testamentum (L) - will; testament.

testate - having made and left a valid will.

testator - one who leaves a valid will.

testatrix - a female testator.

T./et/ G. (Fr) - Tarn/et/ Garonne.

Tex. - Texas.

T. H. - Territory of Hawaii

tho. - *though.

Thomasina (L) - Thomasine Tamsin.

thot. - *thought.

thro. - *through.

tía (Sp) - aunt.

tía abuela (Sp) - grandaunt.

tibicen (L) - fluteplayer; piper.

til - *until.

tila (Fi) - small farm.

Timotheus (L) - Timothy.

tingslag (Sw) - sub-division of a judicial district.

tío (Sp) - uncle.

tío abuelo (Sp) - granduncle.

tipoldefader (D) - 2nd great-grandfather.

Tipp. (Ire) - Tipperary.

tippoldefar (No) - 2nd great-grandfather.

tippoldemor (No) - 2nd great grandmother.

tipp-tippoldefar (No) - 3rd great-grandfather.

tipp-tippoldemor (No) - 3rd great-grandmother.

tipp-tipp-tippoldefar (No) - 4th great-grandfather.

tiptipoldefader (D) - 3rd great-grandfather.

tiptiptipoldefader (D) - 4th great-grandfather.

tithing - a small administrative division locally preserved in many parts of England apparently originally consisting of ten men with their families, or the tenth part of a hundred (q.v.).

tithingman - the chief man of a tithing (q.v.).

tochter (G) - daughter.

tomus (L) - volume; tome; one volume of a larger work. Abbr. - t.

tonsor (L) - barber; haircutter.

Tory - a person living in the American colonies

during the Revolution who remained loyal to Great Britain; a major political party in Great Britain.

town – may refer to an abode or house, a small group of houses, a village, or on up to a large city, according to its usage at various times and places.

township – the inhabitants of, or a vill, manor or medieval town; a social or tribal unit among the Anglo-Saxons; an administrative district similar to a parish; in the U.S., (mostly) a tract of land which is a geographical rather than a political division. Abbr.- tp.; twp.

tp. – township (q.v.).

t.p. – title page.

t.p.m. – title page mutilated

t.p.w. – title page wanting.

Tract Book – a narrative journal like record which is an index to and digest of all essential actions and transactions which effect public lands. District Land Office Tract Books list individual entries by range and township.

tradition – the handing down of statements, beliefs, legends, customs, genealogies, etc., from generation to generation,

esp. by word of mouth.

transcr. – *transcribed.

transcribe – to make a copy of in writing.

transcript – a reproduction in writing or print.

tre (W) – town.

tref (W) – town.

Trenovantum (L) – London.

trial docket – a book or record containing the list of causes to be tried in court.

tritavus (L) – great grandfather's great grandfather.

trolovede (D) – engaged, betrothed.

tr.; trans. – translated, translation.

trustee – orig., a person regarded with trust or to whom something is entrusted; now, one trusted to keep or administer something.

trydydd hendaid (W) – 3rd great-grandfather.

tumulo (L) – to bury; to inter; to entomb.

tumulus (L) – mound; grave; monument; urn.

Tuomiokunta (Fi) – judicial district or judicial circuit.

Turstanus (L) – Thurstan.

Tvl.– Transvaal (So.Africa)

twp. – township (q.v.).

tytär (Fi) – daughter.

tyttärenpoika (Fi) – daughter's son (grandson).

tyttärenpojanpoika (Fi) - daughter's son's son, (great-grandson).

tyttärenpojantyär (Fi) - daughter's son's daughter (great-granddaughter).

tyttärentytär (Fi) - daughter's daughter (granddaughter).

tyttärentyttärenpoika (Fi) - daughter's daughter's son (great-grandson).

tyttö (Fi) - girl.

## U

u. - used interchangeably with "v" in Old English.

uägte (D) - illegitimate.

U. C. - Upper Canada.

uekte (No) - illegitimate.

ugift (D) (No) - unmarried.

U. K. - United Kingdom.

ult. - ultimo (q.v.).

ulter (L) - placed at a greater distance; farther; worse.

ultimo (L) - in the month preceding the present. Abbr. - ult.; ulto.

ultimus - last, end, furthest

ulto. - ultimo (q.v.).

Umfridus (L) - Humfrey.

uncle - a brother of one's mother or father; husband of one's aunt; a familiar title or title of endearment applied to an older man.

uncle-i-l. - *uncle-in-law

(q.v.).

uncle-in-law - the uncle of one's husband or wife; the husband of one's aunt. Abbr. - *uncle-i-l.

unehelich (G) - illegitimate

ungkarl (D) - bachelor.

unigena (L) - only-begotten; only; of one family.

unigenitus (L) - the only son.

union - a registration district in England and Wales, comprising two or more parishes, also called poor-law union.

unit. - *united; *uniting.

unk. - *unknown.

unm. - *unmarried.

unter - (G) - lower.

Unterfr. (G) - Unterfranken

unverheiratet (G) - unmarried.

uomo (It) - man.

urbs (L) - a walled town; city; citizens.

urenkel (G) - great-grandson.

urenkelin (G) - great-granddaughter.

urgrossmutter (G) - great-grandmother.

urgrossvater (G) - great-grandfather.

2ter urgrossvater (G) - 2nd great-grandfather.

3ter urgrossvater (G) - 3rd great-grandfather.

4ter urgrosvater (G) - 4th great-grandfather.

Urovicum (L) - York.

U. S. Postal Guide - the official guide published by the U.S. Post Office, giving the complete list of post offices in the United States and territories. Published yearly. It is called "Directory of Post Offices."

ut (L) - in what manner, how; in the manner that, as; how ever, etc.

ux.; uxor - wife (q.v.).

uxor (L) - wife; spouse; consort. Abbr. - ux.

uxoris (L) - wife.

## V

v - used interchangeably with "u" in Old English.

V., v. - volume.

Va. - Virginia.

v.a. - vixit annos (q.v.).

vader (Du) - father.

Vadum Rubrum (L) - Hertford.

V. Agder. (No) - Vest Agder

vaimo (Fi) - wife.

vanha (Fi) - aged, old.

vanhin (Fi) - eldest.

var. - variation; various.

Varmld. (Sw) - Värmland.

Varvicum (L) - Warwick.

vater (G) - father.

V. Bard. (Ic) - Vestur Bardastrandarsysla.

V. bottn. (Sw) - Västerbotten

vecchio (It) - aged.

vedova (It) - widow.

vedovo (It) - widower.

vel (L) - or; even, even as; at least, etc.

veli (Fi) - brother.

veljenpoka (Fi) - brother's son (nephew).

veljentytär (Fi) - borther's daughter (niece).

Venantodunia (L) - Huntingdonshire.

verbatim - word for word; in the same words; verbally.

verch (W) - daughter (properly merch).

verheiratet (G) - married.

Verovicum (L) - Warwick.

Verouicum (L) - Warwick.

vert, Vert (Her) - green.

Vervicum (L) - Warwick.

Vestfd. (No) - Vestfold.

Vestm. (Ic) - Vestmannaeyjasysla.

vetter (G) - cousin.

vetula (L) - little old woman.

vetulus (L) - little old man.

vetus (L) - aged; old.

veuf (Fr) - widower.

veuve (Fr) - widow.

V. / Hun. (Ic) - Vestur/ Hunavatnssysla.

viator (L) - traveller; a runner or messenger attached to a magistrates service.

vicar - a person acting as priest of a parish in place of a rector; a clergyman.

vicarage - the residence of a vicar; the office or duties of a vicar.

vicaria (L) - vicarage (q.v.)

viculus (L) - little village; hamlet.

vicus (L) - a ward or district of a city; a village; a hamlet.

vide (L) - see.

videlicet (L) - it is easy to see; that is to say; to whit; namely. Abbr. - viz.

video (L) - see.

vidius (L) - living; true to life; vigorous.

vidnere (D) - witnesses.

vidua (L) - widow.

viduata (L) - widowed.

viduus (L) - widower; widow; deprived of or separated from something.

viejo (Sp) - aged.

Vigornia (L) - Worcester.

vil(l)icus (L) - steward; overseer of an estate; balliff; of or belonging to an estate.

village - a small aggregation of houses in the country, being in general less in number than a town or city and more than a hamlet.

village (Fr) - village.

ville (Fr) - city or town.

villie (D) - will.

Villingen (G) - Villingen.

Viluguiana Provincia (L) - Wiltshire.

vintner - one who deals in wine.

vir; viri (L) - man; boy; male; husband; soldier.

virgo (L) - maid; virgin; girl.

viri - see vir.

Vis. - viscount (q.v.) or viscountess.

Visc. - viscount (q.v.). or viscountess.

viscount - an officer who formerly acted in place of the count, or earl; a sheriff. Abbr. - Vis.; Visc; Visct.

Visct. - viscount (q.v). or viscountess.

V./Isf. (Ic) - Vestur/Isafjardarsysla.

visitation - an official personal inquiry made by an officer-at-arms at different times to examine the rights of the people within his heraldic province to bear arms; the record of such inquiry. (see Herald's College, heraldry, etc.).

visitation pedigree - the pedigrees copied by the herald in his book of "visitations" (q.v.).

vital records or statistics - records or statistics relating to birth, deaths, marriages health and disease. Abbr. - *V.R.

viuda (Sp) - widow.

viudo (Sp) - widower.

vivus (L) - alive; living; natural.

vixit annos (L) - he or she lived ___ years. Abbr. -

v.a.

viz. - videlicet.

VL. - Vulgar Latin.

V.ˊManld. (Sw) - Västmanland.

V.ˊNorld. (Sw) - Västernorrland.

vol. - volume.

voorvader (Du) - ancestor, forefather.

Vorarlbg. (Aus) - Vorarlberg.

vorder (G) - anterior.

vorfahre (G) - ancestor, forefather.

v.p. - in father's lifetime.

V.R. - *vital records.

vrouw (Du) - wife.

V.ˊSkaft. (Ic) - Vesturˊ Skaftafellssysla.

Vt. - Vermont.

vuosi (Fi) - year

vixor (L) - wife - see uxor also "V".

## W

w. - wife; *widow.

1/w, 2/w - first wife, second wife, etc.

wald (G) - forest.

Waldsh. (G) - Waldshut.

wapentake - a division corresponding to a hundred and ward (qq.v.) of some Englsih counties; the court of such division; the bailiff serving this court.

ward - in the counties of Cumberland and North- umberland, and in some Scottish counties, a division answering to the hundred and wapentake (qq.v.) of other counties. Wards are often merely or chiefly the divisions of a city for election purposes.

Warewichscira (L) - Warwickshire.

Warning Out Law - a colonial law which empowered a town to warn out individuals or families that were newcomers (within 3 years) and had become impoverished and likely to become town charges, to return to the the town from whence they came. No stigma was attached to this procedure; sometimes a widow with children was warned out after her husbands death, if she did not have means of supporting her family.

Warrant - to guarantee to a purchaser or other grantee, the title to, or quality, or quanitity of, the thing sold or granted, as a warranty deed.

Warwicus (L) - Warwick.

Warws. (E) - Warwick.

Wash. - Washington.

Waterfd. (Ire) - Waterford.

WB. - *Will Book.

wd. - *widow.

weduwe (Du) – widow.

weduwnaar (Du) – widower.

wendisch, windisch (G) – slavic.

Wenta (L) – Monmouth.

west – west, *western.

Westmaria (L) – Westmorland.

Westmd. (E) – Westmorland.

Westmoria, Westmorlandia (L) – Westmorland.

Westph. (G) – Westfalen.

Wexfd. (Ire) – Wexford.

W. Fland. (Bel) – West Vlaanderen.

wf/o – *wife of.

wh. – *who; *which.

Whig – a political party which was in oppositon to the Tories in Great Britain until 1832; also in Colonial America, the Whig Party was opposed to British rule and to the Tories.

Wiccia (L) – Worecestershire.

Wickl. (Ire) – Wicklow.

wid. – *widow.

Wigornia (L) – Worcester.

Wilhelmus (L) – William.

will – the legal declaration of a person's mind as to the manner in which he would have his property or estate disposed of after his death; the term testament (q.v.), originally a Roman and Civil law term, is often now used as synonymous with will. A will or testament may be nuncupative (q.v.) or written. (see SR pp. 12, 13, 16, 17; SYA pp. 11, 84-94; 1953 HB pp. 2, 149, 218; ABC p. 38; GGR pp. 84-89).

Wiltescira, Wiltonia (L) – Wiltshire.

Wilts. (E) – Wiltshire.

windisch (G) – see wendisch

Wis. – Wisconsin.

wit. – *witness, *witnessed.

witness – one who gives testimony as in a court of law; one who signs a document in attestation of the genuineness of its execution; a sponsor at baptism. Abbr. – *wtn.

witwe (G) – widow.

witwer (G) – widower.

wk. – week; work.

wks. – weeks; works.

W. Lothian (Sc) – West Lothian.

W. Meath (Ire) – West Meath

wnt. – *wants.

W/o – *wife of.

Worcs. (E) – Worcester.

WPA Historical Records Survey – a program undertaken by the U.S. Goverment in 1936-43 in which inventories were compiled of historical material, particular unpublished government documents and records which are basic in the administration of local government, and which provide much data for students of political, economic and social history. (see ABC p. 55; 4th Ed HB p. VIII).

W. P. - *will probated.

W. Pruss. (G) - Westpreussen (incl. Danzig).

wtn. - *witness (q.v.).

Wuertt. (G) - Wuerttemberg.

W. Va. - West Virginia.

ww. - *widow.

Ww/O - *widow of.

wwr. - *widower.

Wyo. - Wyoming.

wyr (W) - grandson, grandchild.

wyres (W) - granddaughter.

## X

x - is used to designate an ancestor (q.v.) on some family group sheets

X, - Christ; christian (properly the Greek letter chi. which in form is like X); on pedigrees X is sometimes a symbol for born.

xch - *exchange.

Xn. - Christian.

Xnty. - Christianity.

Xped. - *christened.

Xper.; Xr. - Christopher.

Xpoferus (L) - Christopher.

Xt. - Christ (see X,).

Xtian. - Christian.

Xty. - Christianity.

## Y

y. - year or years.

ye - the (Old English); plural of thou; used for the objective of "you."

yeo - *yeoman; yeomanry (qq.v.).

Yeogerieceastrie (L) - Worcester.

yeoman - a servant, attendant, or subordinate official in royal or other great household; a subordinate of a sheriff; an independant farmer. Abbr. - *yeo.

yeomanry - the position or rank of a yeoman; the collective body of small landed proprietors of the middle class. Abbr. - yeo.

yngst (No) (Sw) - youngest.

yngste (D) - youngest.

Yorks. (E) - Yorkshire.

yr. - year; younger; your.

yrs. - years; yours.

Yukon - Yukon Territory.

## Z

zia (It) - aunt.

zio (It) - uncle.

zittella (It) - girl.

zivilstandsamt (Sz) - place for registration of vital statistics.

zoon (Du) - son.

zuigeling (Du) - infant.

zuster (Du) - sister.

# INDEX

NOTES

## WHY YOU NEED
## "THE HANDY BOOK FOR GENEALOGISTS"

"If I had had the "Handy Book" several years ago it would have saved me many long hours of research and answered thousands of questions I have had to dig out the hard way. Even now I find it to be one of the most used genealogical reference books I own." This was an unsolicited testimonial from a person who has done much professional reserach. Thousands of others have found this same help in their search for ancestors through the information assembled in "The Handy Book for genealogists" by George B. Everton, Sr.

The data it contains is segregated and listed under the 50 States and most of the European Countries. You are given a brief history of each; told when their vital records were started; where their records are kept; who to write to, etc. The counties of each state are listed with the county seat, date of organization, parent county, population, what census reports are available, their libraries and in many cases books are listed telling you where vital information may be had.

You will also find a map of each state showing their counties. As you begin re-

search you will find it is extreemly convenient to know what counties border the one
you are working on as that may give you a
clue as to where to go next.

As an example of how it may help you we
give the following: Your ancestor came from
Hickman, Ky. which is the county seat of
Fulton County. If you turn to page 55 in the
"Handy Book" you find that Fulton County
was formed in 1845 so all records since
that time are found at Hickman. You also
find that Fulton was organized from Hickman, and Hickman was organized from
Caldwell and Livingston in 1821; Calwell
from Livingston in 1809; Livingston from
Christian in 1798; Christian from Logan in
1792; Logan from Lincoln in 1792; and
Lincoln from Kentucky County Va. in 1780.
You also find that Kentucky County Va. was
So designated in December 1776. So you see
you must go to the records of one or more
of these other counties if your progenitor
was there prior to 1845 and you can follow
right on back for each change that was made
almost pin-pointing the place you must look
for his records. Send to THE EVERTON
PUBLISHERS, Box HPO 368, Logan, Utah,
84321, for a free catalogue listing this
book and many other research aids.

## THE GENEALOGICAL HELPER

A quarterly magazine published since 1947, has aided thousands of people all over the world. It is dedicated to helping more people find more genealogy. It is not confined to any particular section of the country but serves people in every state and many foreign countries. It is edited and published by the same concern publishing this book, THE EVERTON PUBLISHERS, HPO Box 368 Logan, Utah, 84321.

Three of the four yearly issues contain not less that thirty six pages, eight-and-a-half by eleven inches. Recent Sept. issues each contain more than two hundred pages. The March issue contains a listing of family associations in the United States with the name and address of the president, and some-times the secretary, of the organization. The June issue contains the addresses of genealogical societies, libraries and professional genealogists in the various states. In each March, June and December issue is a "Question Box" in each one of which generally about sixty or seventy-five researchers ask information on about two hundred fifty or three hundred different families on which they are working.

The easiest way in which to find relatives is to check your family names in "The Genealogists' Exchange" in the various

September issues, which are known as the Annual Exchange Editions, locate the name and address of the registrant or registrants and write them about your problems. These Annual Exchange Editions have been published since 1950.

Hundreds of researchers have extended their pedigrees many generations by utilizing the facilities offered in THE GENE-ALOGICAL HELPER. It is the most widely read genealogical magazine published. Send for a catalogue from THE EVERTON PUBLISHERS Inc., HPO Box 368, Logan, Utah, 84321, listing the subscription price of the "Helper" and many other aids.